MULTINATIONALITY AND FIRM PERFORMANCE

MULTINATIONALITY AND FIRM PERFORMANCE

Ahmed Riahi-Belkaoui

QUORUM BOOKS
WESTPORT, CONNECTICUT • LONDON

Library of Congress Cataloging-in-Publication Data

Riahi-Belkaoui, Ahmed.
Multinationality and firm performance / by Ahmed Riahi-Belkaoui.
p. cm.
Includes bibliographical references and index.
ISBN 1-56720-077-X (alk. paper)
1. International business enterprises. 2. International business enterprises—Finance. 3. Investments, Foreign. I. Title.
HD2755.5.R5 1996
658'.049—dc20 96-15510

British Library Cataloguing in Publication Data is available.

Library of Congress Catalog Card Number: 96-15510
ISBN: 1-56720-077-X

First published in 1996

Quorum Books, 88 Post Road West, Westport, CT 06881
An imprint of Greenwood Publishing Group, Inc.

Printed in the United States of America

The paper used in this book complies with the Permanent Paper Standard issued by the National Information Standards Organization (Z39.48-1984).

10 9 8 7 6 5 4 3 2 1

Copyright Acknowledgments

The author and the publisher gratefully acknowledge permission to use the following:

Material from Sushil Vachani, "Distinguishing between Related and Unrelated International Geographic Diversification: A Comprehensive Measure of Global Diversification," *Journal of International Business Studies* 22, no. 2 (1991): 307–322.

Material from A. L. Calvet, "A Synthesis of Foreign Direct Investment Theories and Theories of the Multinational Firm," *Journal of International Business Studies* (Spring/Summer 1981): 43–59.

Material from John H. Dunning, "Reappraising the Eclectic Paradigm in an Age of Alliance Capitalism," *Journal of International Business Studies* 26, no. 3 (1995): 461–491.

Material from Daniel Sullivan, "Measuring the Degree of Internationalization of a Firm," *Journal of International Business Studies* 25, no. 2 (1994): 325–342.

To Hedi and Janice

Contents

Exhibits

Preface

The world economy is facing new types of capitalism in different parts of the world and a dramatic expansion of foreign direct investment. The key strategy for multinational firms is to be not only strong locally, but also present and thriving internationally. As a result, foreign direct investment of U.S. multinational firms is increasing rapidly. The key questions that emerge from this trend are what is the true nature of multinationality and what are its impacts on firm performance. Both questions are answered in this book by an examination of (a) the nature of multinationality and its alternative measures and (b) the effect of the degree of multinationality on firm performance, where firm performance is expressed by (1) firm value, (2) financial performance, (3) prediction performance of earnings forecasts, (4) diversification strategy and ownership structure, and (5) corporate financing.

This book should be of value to all those interested in international business, finance, and accounting issues, including professional accountants, business executives, teachers and researchers, and students.

Many people helped in the development of this book. I received considerable support from University of Illinois at Chicago research assistants Pearl Zhang and Dimitra Alvertos. I would also like to thank Eric Valentine and Bridget M. Austiguy-Preschel at Greenwood Publishing for their continuous and intelligent support. Finally, to Janice and Hedi, thanks for making everything possible and enjoyable.

MULTINATIONALITY AND FIRM PERFORMANCE

1

The Nature and Degree of Multinationality

INTRODUCTION

The world economy is entering a new phase of market capitalism, taking different forms in different parts of the world. One of the determinants of this new form of market capitalism is the increasing multinationality of firms all over the world. U.S. companies have increased foreign research and development (R&D) spending from $5.2 billion in 1987 to $9.8 billion in 1993. Most of these expenditures were through U.S. affiliates in five countries: Germany, the United Kingdom, Canada, France, and Japan. R&D spending by foreign companies in the United States went from $6.5 billion in 1987 to $14.6 billion in 1993.

Accordingly, this chapter examines the new aspects of this global economy, the role of the multinational corporation in shaping it, and the theory underlying the growing foreign investment decisions of these multinational firms. The chapter also elaborates on the difficulties arising in the definition and measurement of multinationality.

THE GLOBAL ECONOMY

The global economy is best characterized by a new economic and corporate world in which national boundaries are losing their importance. Emerging characteristics of this global economy include the following.

1. A dynamic new world economy in which:

   a. The world will get wealthier with the gross domestic product (GDP) going from $26 trillion (of 1993 dollars) in 1994 to an estimate of $48 trillion in the year 2010.

   b. The world will be more equitable with the GDP of emerging economic nations as share of industrial economies going from 58 percent in 1994 to an estimate of 99 percent in the year 2010.

   c. As developing nations rise, more people will cross the world's borders, emerging markets will become more powerful traders with an emerging market exports as a percent of total world exports going to 30 percent by the year 2010, and new trade and political links may form, with megastates emerging with open regional borders and similar economic systems.

   d. Capital flows will continue to increase beyond the 150 billion global net capital flows in developing countries in 1993, and investment in emerging markets in terms of investment in development economies as a percentage of first world investment will increase from 70 percent to 125 percent in the year 2010.

   e. Technology will be dominant, with a dynamic random access memory (DRAM) capacity in thousands of megabytes per chip going to sixty by the year 2010, and world internet users going from 35 million in 1995 to 180 million by the year 2000.[1]

2. Capitalism will take on many faces: (a) *consumer capitalism* (the United States, Britain, Canada, and Australia) with laissez-faire, open borders, small government, and profit mentality; (b) *producer capitalism* (Germany, France, Japan, and Mexico) with emphasis on production, employment, and statist policies; (c) *family capitalism* (Taiwan, Malaysia, Thailand, and Indonesia) created by Chinese diaspora with extended clans dominating business and capital flows; and (d) *frontier capitalism*

(China and Russia) with government's pursuit of for-profit business ventures and rise of a new entrepreneurial class.[2]

3. There will be greater prosperity with

   a. a smarter labor force characterized by slowing of world population growth from 2.5 percent in 1970 to an estimate of 1.3 percent in the year 2010;
   b. the rise of a new global middle class, for example, in Asia excluding Japan, will rise from 250 in 1994 to 750 million by the year 2010; and
   c. skilled workers becoming numerous, followed by an improvement in wages and incomes.[3]

4. There will be more consumption with

   a. the new affluent buying more cars, with, for example, in the United States sales going from 11.7 million units in 1994 to 13.6 million units in the year 2010;
   b. the new affluent eating out more often, with, for example, the number of McDonald's restaurants worldwide going from 12,000 in 1990 to 20,000 by the year 2000;
   c. the new affluent traveling more widely, with global air traffic in trillions of miles flown by passagers going from 1 in 1985 to over 3 in the year 2010; and
   d. the global use of credit, charge, and debit cards going from $0.10 trillion in 1985 to an estimate of $2 trillion by the year 2010.[4]

5. Partnerships are forming between firms of different nationalities, who are willing to forget their rivalries to share in the profit opportunities of a world market, to share the material and labor costs and risks associated with the development of products, to reduce the impact of fluctuating currencies around the world, and to avoid protectionism and government-imposed obstacles such as tariffs, import limits, and regulations. The most noticeable global strategy emanating from these partnerships is the desire to be present in three major markets—Japan, the United States, and Europe. This strategy, labeled "triad power," consists

of allocating manufacturing, marketing, financing, and administrative operations among the three markets. A similar future strategy is likely to be present in the former socialist countries, given that a frontier capitalism is creating the ground for fuller integration of these countries into the global economy. The frontier capitalism evolves in three stages as follows:

> *Stage one:* statist economies collapse or fadeaway—black marketers profit enormously, with some becoming gangsters. Government corruption spreads.
>
> *Stage two:* small-scale entrepreneurs, often financed by family loans, flouish. Rule of law remains weak but business people start evolving their own rules of commerce.
>
> *Stage three:* economic growth is brisk but hard to measure. Financial markets begin to evolve, tapping savings and attracting foreign institutional investors. Clever legal code appears.[5]

6. Progress is taking place toward international integration in the form of a global capital market. The obstacles to the global capital market remain the persistent existence of different rules concerning regulation of stocks, voting rights, corporate control, antitrust policies, and accounting policies, to name only a few. As more harmonization takes place among nations, the globalization of stocks and common stocks flourish. The evidence of increased globalization relates to the increasing number of stocks markets—by 1992, there were almost two per time zone. The most important markets, forming what is known as the ''Golden Triangle,'' are the New York Stock Exchange (NYSE), the London Stock Exchange (LSE), and the Tokyo Stock Exchange (TSE). These markets open at different times, allowing the great trading houses—Merrill Lynch and Solomons Bros., in the United States; Nomura Securities International, Inc., in Japan; and Bardays Bank, PLC, in the United Kingdom—to trade stocks, bonds, and currencies around the clock and around the world. The building blocks of the next century's markets include Moscow, Prague, Rome, New York, Buenos Aires, Bangkok, and Shanghai. A world of borderless finance will emerge with trillions of dollars and a barrage of financial instruments will whirl around the globe, a world where money and opportunity will know no bounds. A scenario in this new modern finance world follows:

> It's Apr. 20, 2010, a fine spring day in Shanghai. You stroll up to a Citibank automated-teller machine along the Bound, insert your plastic card, and log on. A computer in Bombay greets you, and you get down to business.
>
> First, you shift 10,000 German marks into today's special—an Australian-dollar certificate of deposit issued by GE Capital in Rome. Equities are looking good, so you punch in an order for 500 shares of Telephones de Mexico on the New York Stock Exchange. Then, at the press of a button, an account officer in South Dakota comes onto the screen to answer your questions about a loan for your factory in Argentina.[6]

Other characteristics of this borderless finance would include the fact that with more complex instruments, the markets will become more cruelly efficient and riskier than ever, with global interest rates converging, super currencies emerging, traders vetoing government actions and defeating the very sovereignty of nation states, and a new openness in the form of harmonized accounting and disclosure systems.[7]

In addition, the leaders of tomorrow are the firms that will be using Western-style accounting, Japanese-style teamwork, advanced communication, and freedom and flexibility for entrepreneurial local managers. At the same time to tap economies of scale, they will sell similar products worldwide and offer the same services adapted to local needs in dozens of countries.[8] To be prepared for the next century, firms need to

a. build for speed and flexibility by flattening hierarchies, being on the lookout for joint ventures and partnerships, and using teams to chase down new opportunities and ensure cross-fertilization;

b. be global and local by looking for global products and economies of scale and do not overcentralize; and

c. open up the company by staying open minded, opening information channels, and diversifying management.[9]

7. The rise of the global economy is also evident in the increase in commodity trades and, especially, the creation of big trading blocs. The world seems to be edging toward the following trading blocs:

a. In North America, a trading bloc was created in 1992 by the signing of the North American Free Trade Agreement by the United States, Canada, and Mexico.

b. In Central and South America, trading blocs have been created by (i) the Andean Pact, signed in 1991 by Colombia, Ecuador, Bolivia, Peru, and Venezuela and (ii) the Mercosur Pact, signed in 1991 by Argentina, Brazil, Paraguay, and Uruguay.

c. In Europe, blocs were created by (i) the establishment of the European Community (EC) in 1957 and now consisting of Belgium, Britain, Denmark, France, Germany, Greece, the Netherlands, Ireland, Italy, Luxembourg, Portugal, and Spain and (ii) the European Free Trade Association (EFTA) set up in 1960 by Liechtenstein, Switzerland, Sweden, Finland, Norway, Iceland, and Austria.

d. In Southeast Asia, a bloc was created by the Association of Southeast Asian Nations Free Trade Area, signed in 1992 by Thailand, Indonesia, Malaysia, the Philippines, Singapore, and Brunei. Vietnam and Laos have also expressed interest in joining the pact.

e. In Africa, a bloc was created by the Maghreb countries, an agreement having been signed by Morocco, Algeria, Tunisia, Mauritania, and Libya.

The North American Free Trade Agreement between the United States, Mexico, and Canada was announced in August 1992 as the world's largest trading bloc. The benefits to the U.S. public are best stated as follows:

Consumers: In all three nations, consumers should come out ahead, as tariffs, which raise prices, are lowered and eliminated. Consumers also should find greater choices of goods and services.

Business: Businesses should profit by gaining access to bigger markets and the ability to integrate operations throughout the continent. Some also would benefit by shifting to low-cost production in Mexico.

Labor: The outlook is mixed for American workers. Although as many as 500,000 low-skilled jobs could be transferred to Mexico to save costs, other companies could hire as many U.S. workers to produce products for a modernized Mexico.[10] The agreement is intended to liberalize trade and investment throughout North America.

All these regional trade agreements are the subject of an intense debate. Some subscribe to the idea that these arrangements may lead to (a) an undermining of global free-trade negotiations under the General Agreement on Tariffs and Trade, the 103-nation pact that has set the world's free-trade rules since 1947, and (b) an increase in protectionism as countries use regional agreements to steer business toward their allies, instead of buying from whatever country produces most cheaply.

Some, however, feel that regional free-trade deals are better than no free trade at all, forcing some countries to open their markets to foreign products.

8. In addition to these trading blocs, new economic powers are emerging, especially Japan and the newly unified Germany, to compete head on with the United States.

The key words arising from this new economic order are competitiveness and survival. A new paradigm maintains that competitiveness itself motivates the success of nations. Such is the thesis of Porter, who maintains that the ability of a nation to upgrade its existing advantages to the next level of technology and productivity is the key to international success.[11] Four factors, called the "diamond" of national competitive advantages, are presented as the key to the success of nations:

1. factor conditions (a nation's ability to turn factor endowment into a specialized advantage);
2. demand conditions (the existence of demanding, sophisticated customers);
3. related and supporting industries that provide supplies clusters to firms; and
4. company, strategy, structure, and rivalry (conditions governing how firms in a nation are created and nurtured during times of intense competition).

The differences in competitiveness internationally may be attributed to the differences in corporate ownership and corporate objectives in various parts of the world. In the United States, for example, transient owners such as institutional investors, pension funds, mutual funds, and money managers focus on short-term objectives rather than long-term growth. A 1992 examination of statistics from the stock exchanges in the United States, Japan, and Germany revealed the following differences in corporate ownership:

	United States	Japan	Germany
Individual	30–35%	20%	4%
Institutional owners	2%	40%	27%
Institutional agents	55–60%	6%	3%
Corporations	2–7%	30%	41%
Government	Negligible	Negligible	6%
Foreign investors	6%	4%	19%

Similarly, a 1992 survey by Japan's Economic Planning Agency of 1,000 U.S. and 1,000 Japanese companies revealed the following differences in corporate objectives (the ranking of corporate objects varies from 3 = most important to 0 = least important):

	United States	Japan
Return on investment	2.34	1.24
Higher stock prices	1.14	0.02
Market share	0.73	1.43
Improving and introducing new products	0.71	1.54
Streamlining production and distributing systems	0.46	0.71
Net worth ration	0.38	0.59
Improvement of social image	0.05	0.20
Improvement of working conditions	0.04	0.09

It appears that the American system of capital allocation relies heavily on external capital provided by transient owners comprised of institutional investors, pension funds, mutual funds, and other money managers who are mainly interested in short-term gains. These owners/agents are very motivated by the market performance of their stocks, at the expense of direct interest in the company, its goals, or its level of international competitiveness. As a result, American managers place a higher focus on earning high returns on investments and maximizing current stock prices.

The external and internal capital allocation systems are different in Japan and Germany, where the dominant owners are principals rather than agents who seek long-term growth and have a special relationship with the firm. This special relationship translates into access to inside information and greater influence on managerial behavior.

THE ROLE OF THE MULTINATIONAL CORPORATION

Muller gives the following accurate characterization of the multinational corporations (MNCs):

> The international corporation is emerging. This is a corporation which is internationally owned and controlled. It is not a domestic corporation with some foreign business. It is a business organization with a truly international organization for all its business functions, including management, production, marketing and finance.[12]

It is generally a domestic firm that expanded for the development of a strong product for domestic sales to a complex firm with a multinational management organization and a multinational ownership of equity securities.

An MNC can take one of two forms:

1. a world corporation format that includes the merger of domestic and foreign operations for the functions of research and development, manufacturing, marketing, and finance or
2. an international division format, where all foreign operations are separated from their domestic counterparts in an international division.[13]

The multinational corporation is best viewed as a collection of valuable options.[14] Various benefits can be achieved through the MNC.

First, significant arbitrage benefits can be obtained through

a. exploitation of financing bargains;
b. reduction of taxes on financial flows;
c. the mitigation or shifting of risks to agents with a comparative advantage in bearing them;
d. diversification of cash flows received through foreign operations;
e. the exploitation of various institutional perfection; and
f. the capturing and appropriation of information.

Second, foreign operating options allow additional benefits through

a. location options, which are associated with location alternatives that enhance profits;
b. timing options, which are connected with the exploitation of transient costs and exchange rate disparities;
c. technology options, linking international cost disparities and flexible technologies for the exploitation of the short-term price changes; and
d. staging options, which are associated with establishing a discernible presence in foreign markets.[15]

Finally, other benefits include capital availability and a desirable cost of capital for a considerable range of its capital budget.[16]

FOREIGN INVESTMENT

The multinational corporation is the most developed form of foreign direct investment. The main characteristic is that the foreign segments of the operations are not only owned but managed by the parent firm. A direct foreign investment involves the transfer of capital, managerial, and technical assets of a firm from one country (the home country) to another (the host country) by (within) the same firm. The opposite of a direct foreign investment is a foreign portfolio investment. Although direct foreign investment implies control over the subsidiary, foreign portfolio investment implies a purely financial investment in foreign securities, either bonds or equities purchased in small amounts to create no controlling will in the (foreign) firms involved.

Direct foreign investment is undertaken after an evaluation of the role and return of the foreign project and of the potential managerial presence of the parent firm in the host country. Foreign portfolio investment limits the analysis to the risk/return consideration.

Firms engage in foreign direct investment and expand their markets by producing and selling abroad. Some of the reasons include the following:

- to reduce transportation costs;
- because of a lack of domestic policy;
- to achieve economies of scale in small-scale process technology;
- to avoid trade or customer-imposed restrictions;
- to follow customers and competitors;
- to benefit from a different cost structure;
- to rationalize production by taking advantage of varying costs of labor, capital, and raw materials;
- to have access to production factors;
- to take advantage of government investment incentives;
- because of political motives;
- to use monopoly advantage over similar companies in the foreign countries; and
- to have better profitability and stable sales and earnings.[17,18]

Arguments against foreign investment include the following:

1. Foreign investment brings about the loss of political and economic sovereignty.
2. It controls key industries and export markets.
3. It exploits local natural resources and unskilled workers.
4. It undermines indigenous cultures and societies by imposing Western values and lifestyle in developing countries.[19]

Firms making foreign investment decisions have been classified as

1. market seekers,
2. raw material seekers,
3. production efficiency seekers,
4. knowledge seekers, and/or
5. political safety seekers.[20]

After making a decision in direct foreign investment, the multinational firm still must decide on a model of foreign entry. The main choices are

1. a joint venture with one or more local parties
2. a 100%-owned greenfield (newly established) foreign subsidiary
3. a merger with an acquisition of an estimating local firm
4. a strategies alliance with one or more foreign partners.[21]

Various models and theories can be used to explain foreign direct investment. They include the international trade theory, the location theory, and the investment theory view.

The international trade theory focuses on either a comparative cost view, whereby the investment is justified by cost consideration, or the product life cycle view, whereby the investment is justified by a stage of the product that makes it attractive to foreign buyers.

The location theory focuses on the location options as a determinant of the investment.

The investment theory focuses either on an imperfect capital markets view, whereby imperfections in the foreign capital markets favor the investment, or the portfolio of foreign direct investment view, whereby the investment allows some risk diversification.

Although the conventional wisdom argues for an eclectic approach to explain foreign direct investment, the internalization view holds some interest. Basically, it argues that firms having a competitive advantage caused by their ability to generate proprietary information can benefit from these innovations through direct foreign investment.

In fact, the eclectic theory and the internalization approach are similar because they postulate that the existence of firm-specific, or ''ownership,'' advantages and country-specific, or ''location,'' advantages do not fully explain the foreign investment decision, because there must also exist some advantage to ''internalizing'' the foreign venture. An excellent review of all these theories is provided in Appendix 1.A. More recently, Dunning[22] noticed the change from a situation where the development of resources and capabilities in market-oriented economics are shaped by a micro-organizational system known as fordism and a macro-institutional system known as hierarchical capitalism[23] to alliance, relational, collective, associate, or ''new'' capitalism, where the organization of production and transactions involve both cooperation and competition between the leading wealth agents. As a result of the shift, a reconfiguration of the eclectic paradigm of international production is proposed, as shown in Exhibit 1.1. The left-hand side of the exhibit shows the hierarchical-related advantages and the right-hand side presents the alliance or network-related advantages.

DEGREE OF MULTINATIONALITY

Estimating the degree of multinationality of a firm has led to a choice of different measures. One innovative and original measure of the degree of multinationality is inferred from a firm's gradual acquisition, integration and use of knowledge about foreign markets and operations, and the incrementally increasing commitments to foreign markets.[24]

From an examination of the literature, Sullivan[25] identified three attributes of the degree of multinationality:

1. performance in terms of what goes on overseas,[26]
2. structure in terms of what resources are used overseas,[27] and
3. attitude or conduct in terms of what is the top management orientation.[28]

In terms of performance, five measures have been used to operationalize multinationality: (1) foreign sales as a percentage of total sales (FSTS),[29] (2) research and development intensity (RDI),[30] (3) advertising intensity (AI),[31] (4) export sales as a percentage of total sales

Exhibit 1.1
A Reconfiguration of the Eclectic Paradigm of International Production

1. Ownership-Specific Advantages
(of enterprise of one nationality (or affiliates of same) over those of another)

Hierarchical-Related Advantages

a. Property right and/or intangible asset advantages (Oa).

Product innovations, production management, organizational and marketing systems, innovatory capacity, non-codifiable knowledge: "bank" of human capital experience; marketing, finance, know-how, etc.

b. Advantages of common governance, i.e., of organizing Oa with complementary assets (Ot).

(i) Those that branch plants of established enterprises may enjoy over de novo firms. Those due mainly to size, product diversity and learning experiences of enterprise, e.g., economies of scope and specialization. Exclusive or favored access to inputs, e.g., labor, natural resources, finance, information. Ability to obtain inputs on favored terms (due, e.g., to size or monopsonistic influence). Ability of parent company to conclude productive and cooperative inter-firm relationships e.g., as between Japanese auto assemblers and their suppliers. Exclusive or favored access to product markets. Access to resources of parent company at marginal cost. Synergistic economies (not only in production, but in purchasing, marketing, finance, etc., arrangements).

(ii) Which specifically arise because of multinationality. Multinationality enhances operational flexibility by offering wider opportunities for arbitraging, production shifting and global sourcing of inputs. More favored access to and/or better knowledge about international markets, e.g., for information, finance, labor etc. Ability to take advantage of geographic differences in factor endowments, government intervention, markets, etc. Ability to diversify or reduce risks, e.g., in different currency areas, and creation of options and/or political and cultural scenarios. Ability to learn from societal differences in organizational and managerial processes and systems. Balancing economies of integration with ability to respond to differences in country-specific needs and advantages.

Alliance or Network-Related Advantages

a. *Vertical Alliances*

(i) Backward access to R&D, design engineering and training facilities of suppliers. Regular input by them on problem solving and product innovation on the consequences of projected new production processes for component design and manufacturing. New insights into, and monitoring of, developments in materials, and how they might impact on existing products and production processes.

(ii) Forward access to industrial customers, new markets, marketing techniques and distribution channels, particularly in unfamiliar locations or where products need to be adapted to meet local supply capabilities and markets. Advice by customers on product design and performance. Help in strategic market positioning.

b. *Horizontal Alliances*

Access to complementary technologies and innovatory capacity. Access to additional capabilities to capture benefits of technology fusion, and to identify new uses for related technologies. Encapsulation of learning and development times. Such inter-firm interaction often generates its own knowledge feedback mechanisms and path dependencies.

c. *Networks*

(i) of similar firms
Reduced transaction and coordination costs arising from better dissemination and interpretation of knowledge and information, and from mutual support and cooperation between members of network. Improved knowledge about process and product development and markets. Multiple, yet complementary, inputs into innovatory developments and exploitation of new markets. Access to embedded knowledge of members of networks. Opportunities to develop 'niche' R&D strategies; shared learning and training experiences, e.g., as in the case of cooperative research associations. Networks may also help promote uniform product standards and other collective advantages.

(ii) business districts
As per (i) plus spatial agglomerative economies, e.g., labor market pooling. Access to clusters of specialized intermediate inputs, and linkages with knowledge-based institutions, e.g., universities, technological spill-overs.

Exhibit 1.1 (Continued)

2. Internalization Incentive Advantages (i.e., to circumvent or exploit market failure).

Hierarchical-Related Advantages	Alliance or Network-Related Advantages
Avoidance of search and negotiating costs. To avoid costs of moral hazard, information asymmetries and adverse selection; and to protect reputation of internalizing firm. To avoid cost of broken contracts and ensuing litigation. Buyer uncertainty (about nature and value of inputs (e.g., technology) being sold). When market does not permit price discrimination. Need of seller to protect quality of intermediate or final products. To capture economies of interdependent activities (see b. above). To compensate for absence of future markets. To avoid or exploit government intervention (e.g., quotas, tariffs, price controls, tax differences, etc.) To control supplies and conditions of sale of inputs (including technology). To control market outlets (including those which might be used by competitors). To be able to engage in practices, e.g., cross-subsidization, predatory pricing, leads and lags, transfer pricing, etc. as a competitive (or anti-competitive) strategy.	While, in some cases, time limited inter-firm cooperative relationships may be a substitute for FDI; in others, they may add to the I incentive advantages of the participating hierarchies, R&D alliances and networking which may help strengthen the overall competitiveness of the participating firms. Moreover, the growing structural integration of the world economy is requiring firms to go outside their immediate boundaries to capture the complex realities of know-how trading and knowledge exchange in innovation, particularly where intangible assets are tacit and need to speedily adapt competitive enhancing strategies to structural change. Alliances or network related advantages are those which prompt a 'voice' rather than an 'exit' response to market failure; they also allow many of the advantages of internalization without the inflexibility, bureaucratic or risk-related costs associated with it. Such quasi-internalization is likely to be most successful in cultures in which trust, forbearances, reciprocity and consensus politics are at a premium. It suggests that firms are more appropriately likened to archipelagos linked by causeways rather than self-contained 'islands' of conscious power. At the same time, flagship or lead MNEs, by orchestrating the use of mobile O advantages and immobile advantages, enhance their role as arbitragers of complementary cross-border value-added activities.

3. Location-Specific Variables (these may favor home or host countries)

Hierarchical-Related Advantages	Alliance or Network-Related Advantages
Spatial distribution of natural and created resource endowments and markets. Input prices, quality and productivity, e.g. labor, energy, materials, components, semi-finished goods. International transport and communication costs. Investment incentives and disincentives (including performance requirements, etc.). Artificial barriers (e.g. import controls) to trade in goods. Societal and infrastructure provisions (commercial, legal, educational, transport, and communication). Cross-country ideological, language, cultural, business, political, etc. differences. Economies of centralization of R&D production and marketing. Economic system and policies of government: the institutional framework for resource allocation.	The L-specific advantages of alliances arise essentially from the presence of a portfolio of immobile local complementary assets, which, when organized within a framework of alliances and networks, produce a stimulating and productive industrial atmosphere. The extent and type of business districts, industrial or science parks and the external economies they offer participating firms are examples of these advantages which over time may allow foreign affiliates and cross-border alliances and network relationships to better tap into, and exploit, the comparative technological and organizational advantages of host countries. Networks may also help reduce the information asymmetries and likelihood of opportunism in imperfect markets. They may also create local institutional thickness, intelligent regions and social embeddedness [Amin and Thrift 1994].

Source: John H. Dunning, "Reappraising the Eclectic Paradigm in an Age of Alliance Capitalism," *Journal of International Business Studies* 26, no.3 (1995): 475–476. Reprinted with permission.

(ESTS),[32] and (5) foreign profits as a percentage of total profits (FPTP).[33]

In terms of structure, two measures of multinationality have been used: (1) foreign assets as a percentage of total assets (FATA)[34] and (2) overseas subsidiaries as a percentage of total subsidiaries (OSTS).

In terms of conduct, two measures of multinationality have been used: (1) top management's international experience (TMIE) as the cumulative duration of top management's international assignments weighted by the reported total numbers of years of work experience of the top management team of the firm[35] and (2) the psychic dispersion of international operations (PDIO)[36] by calibrating the dispersion of subsidiaries of a firm among the following ten psychic zones as identified by Ronen and Shenkar[37]: Anglo, Germanic, Nordic, Near Eastern, Arab, Far Eastern, Latin American, Latin European, Independent, and other.

Of these nine measures, an item-total analysis showed the five variables FSTS, FATA, OSTS, PDIO, and TMIE to have a high reliability in the construction of a homogeneous measure of multinationality.[38] A conclusion of these five measures into a measure called ''Degree of Internationalization Scale'' (DOI_{INTS}) is computed as follows:

$$DOI_{INTS} = \text{FSTS} + \text{FATA} + \text{OSTS} + \text{PDIO} + \text{TMIE}.$$

DOI_{INTS} for the 1979–1990 ''most international'' 100 American manufacturing and service firms identified by *Forbes* is shown in Exhibit 1.2. Company ranking on six estimators of the degree of internationalization of a firm, as shown in Exhibit 1.3, suggest that DOI_{INTS} is another good measure of multinationality, but not necessarily a better measure of multinationality. For example, Pfizer, which is scaled twenty-second and thirty-first in terms of FSTS and FATA is strangely seventh in terms of DOI. Other examples could be used before an indiscriminate use of DOI_{INTS}.

THE MOST INTERNATIONAL FIRMS

Since 1979, *Forbes* has published a best of the ''Most International'' 100 American manufacturing and service firms. They were ranked on the basis of foreign revenues. This chapter relies on the classification from 1986 to 1994. Descriptive statistics on the total sample are shown

Exhibit 1.2
Sample Company's Value on the Measurement Scale of DOI_{INTS}

Company	DOI_{INTS}	Company	DOI_{INTS}
1. CPC	3.13	38. Albbot	2.10
2. Exxon	3.02	39. Allied Signal	2.10
3. Colgate-Palmolive	2.97	40. Caterpillar	2.08
4. IBM	2.91	41. Kimberly Clark	2.08
5. Gillette	2.90	42. Borden	2.00
6. Mobil	2.86	43. Philip Morris	2.00
7. Pfizer	2.83	44. Alcoa	1.97
8. American Brands	2.82	45. Dresser	1.95
9. DEC	2.81	46. Emerson Electric	1.94
10. Hewlett Packard	2.77	47. Union Carbide	1.94
11. Dow Chemical	2.75	48. Amoco	1.92
12. Merck	2.65	49. PPG	1.91
13. Johnson&Johnson	2.62	50. Quaker Oats	1.90
14. Coca-Cola	2.61	51. General Motors	1.88
15. Eli Lilly	2.59	52. Scott Paper	1.82
16. AMP	2.58	53. Rockwell Int'l	1.81
17. Avon	2.50	54. WR Grace	1.81
18. Motorola	2.45	55. Deere	1.75
19. Warner Lambert	2.45	56. Tenneco	1.74
20. Black & Decker	2.44	57. TRW	1.64
21. NCR	2.43	58. Baxter Travenol	1.64
22. Texaco	2.35	59. Sara Lee	1.63
23. 3M	2.33	60. Pepsi Cola	1.57
24. Procter & Gamble	2.32	61. Ralston-Purina	1.57
25. American Cyanamid	2.31	62. International Paper	1.54
26. Goodyear	2.31	63. United Technologies	1.52
27. Unisys	2.30	64. Chevron	1.51
28. Heinz	2.29	65. Honeywell	1.44
29. Bristol-Myers	2.29	66. Xerox	1.38
30. Kellogg	2.27	67. Whirlpool	1.38
31. Eastman-Kodak	2.25	68. Atlantic Richfield	1.18
32. Intel	2.23	69. Westinghouse	1.13
33. Monsanto	2.17	70. General Electric	1.06
34. Ford	2.14	71. Phillips Petroleum	1.00
35. E.I. Dupont	2.14	72. Chrysler	.94
36. Amer Home Products	2.13	73. Unocal	.91
37. Texas Instruments	2.12	74. Sun	.54

Notes: The five variables constituting DOI_{INTS}—*FSTS, FATA, OSTS, PDIO,* and *TMIE*—are ratio variables. As such, the range of value for a firm is 0.0 (absolutely no international involvement) to 5.0 (absolutely total international involvement). We calculate a firm's score through the following operation:

$$FSTS + FATA + OSTS + PDIO + TMIE = DOI_{INTS}.$$

So, for example, IBM's value of 2.91 for DOI_{INTS} was derived accordingly:

$$.59_{FSTS} + .50_{FATA} + .77_{OSTS} + .9_{PDIO} + .15_{TMIE} = 2.91.$$

Source: Daniel Sullivan, "Measuring the Degree of Internationalization of a Firm," *Journal of International Business Studies* 25, no. 2. (1994): 335. Reprinted with permission.

Exhibit 1.3
Company Rankings on Six Estimators of the Degree of Internationalization of a Firm

Company	DOI_{INTS}	*FSTS*	*FATA*	*OSTS*	*TMIE*	*PDIO*
CPC	1	12	9	14	1	1
Exxon	2	1	1	26	26	28
Colgate Palmolive	3	3	3	28	19	20
IBM	4	6	10	8	21	15
Gillette	5	2	2	19	10	46
Mobil	6	4	8	49	7	1
Pfizer	7	22	31	4	2	18
American Brands	6	15	11	1	38	17
DEC	9	9	7	3	25	43
Hewlett Packard	10	12	20	5	29	19
Dow Chemical	11	8	5	31	16	14
Merck	12	17	30	9	13	17
Johnson & Johnson	13	14	14	11	70	21
Coca-Cola	14	6	4	35	31	39
Eli Lilly	15	33	25	2	23	8
AMP	16	10	16	7	57	38
Avon	17	8	6	38	14	48
Motorola	18	13	29	13	43	41
Warner Lambert	19	18	40	12	5	57
Black & Decker	20	23	13	37	15	40
NCR	21	4	17	15	35	62
Texaco	22	20	64	51	6	1
3M	23	21	25	46	9	35
Procter & Gamble	24	39	51	23	3	34
American Cyanamid	25	28	23	33	22	37

Source: Daniel Sullivan, ''Measuring the Degree of Internationalization of a Firm,'' *Journal of International Business Studies* 25, no. 2 (1994): 336. Reprinted with permission.

in Exhibit 1.4. Of interest to the study is the level of multinationality as measured by (a) foreign profits/total profits, (b) foreign revenues/total revenues, and (c) foreign assets/total assets. They show a high level and range of multinationality among these U.S. firms. Exhibit 1.5 shows foreign revenues/total revenues for all these firm from 1986 to 1994. It appear that Exxon, Mobil, and IBM keep the first, second, and third ranks for the whole period of study. Citicorp started sixth and very quickly moved to and stayed at the fourth rank, then shared the same rank as IBM. Other companies that are moving fast in terms of foreign/total

Exhibit 1.4
Descriptive Statistics

1.Simple Statistics

Variable	Mean	Std Dev	Sum	Minimum	Maximum
C	37.4526	15.8514	25992	6.6000	93.0000
D	52.8162	59.7152	31214	0.2000	914.3000
E	769.7911	1200	534235	-7987	6020
F	39.9213	202.1856	27027	2.7000	5280
G	29626	43943	20560708	56.4000	251506
H	4997	6554	4137681	-438.0000	84145
I	10433	12456	8638568	283.6000	83584
J	95.9053	2718	79410	0	78221
R	0.0761	0.0619	37.7692	0.001101	0.3498

2. Variable definition

c= Foreign Revenues/Total Revenues.
d= Foreign Profit/Total Profit.
e= Total Profit.
f= Foreign Assets/Total Assets.
g= Total Assets.
h= Book Value of Equity.
i= Market Value of Equity.
j=Dividend Rate.
r=Rate of Return on Assets.

Exhibit 1.4 (Continued)

. Univariate Procedure

.1 Variable=C

Moments

N		Sum Wgts	694
Mean	37.45259	Sum	25992.1
Std Dev	15.85141	Variance	251.2673
Skewness	0.356839	Kurtosis	-0.19127
USS	1147600	CSS	174128.3
CV	42.32394	Std Mean	0.601711
T:Mean=0	62.24345	Pr>|T|	0.0001
Num ¬= 0	694	Num > 0	694
M(Sign)	347	Pr>=|M|	0.0001
Sgn Rank	120582.5	Pr>=|S|	0.0001

Quantiles(Def=5)

100% Max	93	99%	76.8
75% Q3	47.4	95%	66.5
50% Med	36.7	90%	59
25% Q1	25.7	10%	17.2
0% Min	6.6	5%	12.9
		1%	7.5
Range	86.4		
Q3-Q1	21.7		
Mode	36.1		

Extremes

Lowest	Obs	Highest	Obs
6.6(	852)	77.7(	312)
6.9(	320)	77.7(	332)
7(	54)	79.8(	179)
7.1(	187)	82.5(	46)
7.5(	787)	93(	1)

Exhibit 1.4 (Continued)

```
Univariate Procedure

.2.Variable=D

                         Moments

N                          Sum Wgts         591
Mean         52.81624      Sum          31214.4
Std Dev      59.71517      Variance    3565.902
Skewness     7.127994      Kurtosis    82.43857
USS           3752510      CSS          2103882
CV           113.0621      Std Mean    2.456354
T:Mean=0     21.50189      Pr>|T|        0.0001
Num ¬= 0          591      Num > 0          591
M(Sign)         295.5      Pr>=|M|       0.0001
Sgn Rank        87468      Pr>=|S|       0.0001


                    Quantiles(Def=5)

100% Max         914.3          99%       295.9
 75% Q3           61.9          95%       127.8
 50% Med          41.3          90%        86.5
 25% Q1             25          10%          14
  0% Min           0.2           5%         9.8
                                 1%           3
Range            914.1
Q3-Q1             36.9
Mode              22.9


                         Extremes

     Lowest      Obs       Highest      Obs
        0.2(      320)        310(       640)
        0.3(       54)      315.9(       541)
        2.2(      852)      410.3(        53)
        2.8(      843)      505.4(       416)
        2.8(      719)      914.3(       465)
```

Exhibit 1.4 (Continued)

3.3 Variable=E

Moments

N		Sum Wgts	694
Mean	769.7911	Sum	534235
Std Dev	1199.824	Variance	1439578
Skewness	0.382845	Kurtosis	10.66344
USS	1.4089E9	CSS	9.9763E8
CV	155.8636	Std Mean	45.5447
T:Mean=0	16.90188	Pr>|T|	0.0001
Num ¬= 0	694	Num > 0	619
M(Sign)	272	Pr>=|M|	0.0001
Sgn Rank	100950	Pr>=|S|	0.0001

Quantiles(Def=5)

100% Max	6020	99%	5360
75% Q3	1096	95%	2881
50% Med	543	90%	1918
25% Q1	245	10%	-53
0% Min	-7987	5%	-417
		1%	-2258
Range	14007		
Q3-Q1	851		
Mode	98		

Extremes

Lowest	Obs	Highest	Obs
-7987(	4)	5491(	669)
-6865(	137)	5600(	267)
-4992(	268)	5703(	546)
-2621(	135)	5950(	679)
-2567(	187)	6020(	403)

Exhibit 1.4 (Continued)

3.4.Variable=F

Moments

N		Sum Wgts	677
Mean	39.92127	Sum	27026.7
Std Dev	202.1856	Variance	40879.01
Skewness	25.82824	Kurtosis	670.3641
USS	28713152	CSS	27634212
CV	506.4608	Std Mean	7.770623
T:Mean=0	5.13746	Pr>|T|	0.0001
Num ¬= 0	677	Num > 0	677
M(Sign)	338.5	Pr>=|M|	0.0001
Sgn Rank	114751.5	Pr>=|S|	0.0001

Quantiles(Def=5)

100% Max	5280	99%	82.1
75% Q3	41.4	95%	57.5
50% Med	30.5	90%	48.9
25% Q1	22.6	10%	15.5
0% Min	2.7	5%	11
		1%	3.6
Range	5277.3		
Q3-Q1	18.8		
Mode	19.8		

Extremes

Lowest	Obs	Highest	Obs
2.7(	320)	84.7(	509)
3(	852)	86.6(	312)
3(	54)	87.1(	179)
3.1(	187)	88.4(	46)
3.4(	453)	5280(	1)

Exhibit 1.4 (Continued)

3.5.Variable=G

Moments

N		Sum Wgts	694
Mean	29626.38	Sum	20560708
Std Dev	43942.55	Variance	1.9309E9
Skewness	2.501556	Kurtosis	6.315729
USS	1.947E12	CSS	1.338E12
CV	148.3224	Std Mean	1668.036
T:Mean=0	17.76123	Pr>|T|	0.0001
Num ¬= 0	694	Num > 0	694
M(Sign)	347	Pr>=|M|	0.0001
Sgn Rank	120582.5	Pr>=|S|	0.0001

Quantiles(Def=5)

100% Max	251506	99%	207106
75% Q3	32346	95%	137682
50% Med	10335.5	90%	87241
25% Q1	5263	10%	3858
0% Min	56.4	5%	2976
		1%	1958
Range	251449.6		
Q3-Q1	27083		
Mode	3261		

Extremes

Lowest	Obs	Highest	Obs
56.4(	1)	221897(	273)
833(	92)	225801(	140)
922(	225)	228240(	7)
981(	358)	231788(	406)
1729(	348)	251506(	14)

Exhibit 1.4 (Continued)

3.6.Variable=H

Moments

N		Sum Wgts	828
Mean	4997.199	Sum	4137681
Std Dev	6553.815	Variance	42952496
Skewness	4.464606	Kurtosis	32.85632
USS	5.62E10	CSS	3.552E10
CV	131.1498	Std Mean	227.7608
T:Mean=0	21.94056	Pr>|T|	0.0001
Num ¬= 0	827	Num > 0	823
M(Sign)	409.5	Pr>=|M|	0.0001
Sgn Rank	171128	Pr>=|S|	0.0001

Quantiles(Def=5)

100% Max	84145	99%	34473.6
75% Q3	5529.65	95%	16214.4
50% Med	2963.95	90%	10835.2
25% Q1	1744.2	10%	994
0% Min	-438	5%	648
		1%	152.5
Range	84583		
Q3-Q1	3785.45		
Mode	982.8		

Extremes

Lowest	Obs	Highest	Obs
-438(	645)	37289.7(	669)
-283.6(	778)	38200.8(	536)
-237.6(	457)	38297.2(	270)
-138.8(	911)	40548.1(	403)
0(	584)	84145(	1)

Exhibit 1.4 (Continued)

3.7.Variable=I

Moments

N		Sum Wgts	828
Mean	10433.05	Sum	8638568
Std Dev	12456.31	Variance	1.5516E8
Skewness	2.720786	Kurtosis	8.688811
USS	2.184E11	CSS	1.283E11
CV	119.3927	Std Mean	432.8866
T:Mean=0	24.10112	Pr>|T|	0.0001
Num ¬= 0	828	Num > 0	828
M(Sign)	414	Pr>=|M|	0.0001
Sgn Rank	171603	Pr>=|S|	0.0001

Quantiles(Def=5)

100% Max	83584.2	99%	65105.4
75% Q3	12416.2	95%	34699.3
50% Med	5844	90%	24322.5
25% Q1	3220.5	10%	1795.4
0% Min	283.6	5%	1287
		1%	646.8
Range	83300.6		
Q3-Q1	9195.7		
Mode	719.1		

Extremes

Lowest	Obs	Highest	Obs
283.6(	778)	72368(	144)
382.5(	393)	73325.2(	267)
425(	526)	74255.5(	29)
438(	645)	74490(	134)
485.7(	449)	83584.2(	14)

Exhibit 1.4 (Continued)

3.8.Variable=J

Moments

N		Sum Wgts	828
Mean	95.90528	Sum	79409.57
Std Dev	2718.311	Variance	7389214
Skewness	28.77498	Kurtosis	827.9998
USS	6.1185E9	CSS	6.1109E9
CV	2834.371	Std Mean	94.46784
T:Mean=0	1.015216	Pr>|T|	0.3103
Num ¬= 0	746	Num > 0	746
M(Sign)	373	Pr>=|M|	0.0001
Sgn Rank	139315.5	Pr>=|S|	0.0001

Quantiles(Def=5)

100% Max	78220.8	99%	4.84
75% Q3	2	95%	3.2
50% Med	1.32	90%	2.8
25% Q1	0.75	10%	0.02
0% Min	0	5%	0
		1%	0
Range	78220.8		
Q3-Q1	1.25		
Mode	0		

Extremes

Lowest	Obs	Highest	Obs
0(	925)	5(	800)
0(	923)	5.5(	39)
0(	911)	5.5(	172)
0(	895)	5.5(	305)
0(	888)	78220.8(	1)

Exhibit 1.4 (Continued)

3.9.Variable=R

Moments

N		Sum Wgts	496
Mean	0.076147	Sum	37.76915
Std Dev	0.06186	Variance	0.003827
Skewness	1.21526	Kurtosis	1.507629
USS	4.770208	CSS	1.894182
CV	81.23677	Std Mean	0.002778
T:Mean=0	27.415	Pr>|T|	0.0001
Num ¬= 0	496	Num > 0	496
M(Sign)	248	Pr>=|M|	0.0001
Sgn Rank	61628	Pr>=|S|	0.0001

Quantiles(Def=5)

100% Max	0.349758	99%	0.278279
75% Q3	0.10374	95%	0.198882
50% Med	0.063229	90%	0.166804
25% Q1	0.026516	10%	0.009132
0% Min	0.001101	5%	0.005513
		1%	0.002078
Range	0.348657		
Q3-Q1	0.077224		
Mode	0.16958		

Extremes

Lowest	Obs	Highest	Obs
0.001101(	824)	0.278279(	171)
0.001331(	559)	0.278863(	869)
0.001439(	539)	0.282482(	173)
0.001918(	647)	0.311853(	872)
0.002078(	698)	0.349758(	863)

Exhibit 1.5
Foreign Revenues as a Percentage of Total Revenues

	Name	1986	1987	1988	1989	1990	1991	1992	1993	1994
1.	Exxon	72.0%	75.%	71.6%	73.2%	74.9%	75.9%	76.8%	77.3%	77.4%
2.	Mobil	59.5%	60.5%	67.1%	64.7%	55.3%	68.1%	68.1%	67.5%	67.6%
3.	IBM	50.5%	54.0%	57.6%	58.9%	60.7%	62.3%	61.8%	59.0%	62.3%
4.	Ford Motor	31.8%	32.8%	45.3%	33.2%	36.7%	39.1%	35.7%	30.3%	29.6%
5.	General Motors	19.3%	23.7%	24.3%	26.6%	30.3%	31.8%	32.0%	28.0%	28.4%
6.	Texaco	49.0%	49.8%	48.7%	42.3%	42.8%	49.9%	52.6%	53.5%	55.9%
7.	Citicorp	46.6%	48.4%	51.4%	52.3%	54.9%	52.9%	60.3%	64.5%	62.3%
8.	El du Pont de Nernours	37.0%	38.2%	39.2%	39.8%	43.5%	44.8%	46.9%	51.4%	42.1%
9.	Dow Chemical	53.5%	55.6%	55.1%	54.1%	52.0%	51.7%	49.7%	48.6%	50.3%
10.	Chevron	23.0%	22.7%	20.9%	20.5%	22.3%	38.2%	44.1%	41.1%	42.9%
11.	Bank America	37.3%	31.3%	29.1%	28.1%	23.5%	20.9%	17.4%	17.9%	19.8%
12.	Philip Morris	22.1%	20.4%	20.3%	19.6%	23.6%	27.4%	27.7%	30.3%	30.4%
13.	Proctor & Gamble	29.1%	32.5%	37.7%	39.9%	39.9%	45.6%	49.7%	52.1%	51.7%
14.	RJR Nabisco	28.1%	25.7%	-	-	14.0%	18.1%	18.8%	27.8%	30.9%

Exhibit 1.5 (Continued)

15.	Chase Manhattan	46.0%	46.7%	49.2%	43.2%	38.7%	37.0%	45.0%	48.6%	39.9%
16.	ITT	24.0%	25.0%	43.0%	43.3%	45.2%	30.9%	30.3%	32.6%	33.0%
17.	Eastman Kodak	35.9%	39.6%	41.2%	40.9%	43.6%	44.0%	43.5%	48.8%	52.5%
18.	Coca-Cola	46.4%	54.7%	55.4%	54.5%	61.2%	64.0	66.5%	67.0%	68.3%
19.	Xerox	30.6%	32.1%	34.9%	34.6%	42.2%	44.3%	45.6%	47.6%	47.8%
20.	Amoco	21.3%	21.5%	22.6%	26.1%	28.2%	24.8%	23.6%	22.3%	21.7%
21.	General Electric	10.4%	9.4%	9.2%	12.4%	14.2%	14.4%	16.9%	16.6%	19.8%
22.	United Technologies	24.3%	27.4%	28.5%	32.9%	36.0%	37.8%	39.5%	38.7%	39.2%
23.	JP Morgan	54.8%	52.5%	52.9%	47.0%	45.4%	48.2%	50.6%	52.4%	45.6%
24.	Good Year	37.9%	40.4%	43.8%	40.9%	42.7%	42.9%	42.4%	41.8%	42.0%
25.	Hewlett -Packard	46.3%	49.0%	51.60%	53.3%	54.5%	54.2%	56.1%	54.0%	54.1%
26.	American Express	22.1%	19.8%	18.8%	19.4%	22.0%	20.00%	20.3%	29.5%	27.6%
27.	Minn Mining & Mfg	37.4%	38.3%	40.0%	44.9%	47.8%	48.5%	49.0%	49.2%	50.2%
28.	Unisys	42.9%	43.6%	45.8%	49.1%	51.8%	51.0%	50.7%	47.4%	50.9%
29.	Tenneco	21.5%	25.9%	30.3%	30.4%	31.2%	28.9%	27.6%	25.4%	22.0%

30.	Digital Equipment	41.1%	46.6%	49.4%	54.1%	55.0%	59.8%	63.0%	63.7%	61.5%
31.	Johnson & Johnson	43.3%	48.0%	49.2%	50.0%	51.7%	49.8%	49.8%	49.1%	50.3%
32.	American Int'l Corp	33.8%	34.4%	36.6%	38.4%	40.2%	43.4%	44.9%	50.4%	.51.8%
33.	Sears Roebuck	6.6%	6.6%	7.5%	7.7%	7.5%	6.9%	7.1%	7.0%	6.7%
34.	CPC International	63.1%	45.1%	56.5%	55.7%	59.8%	62.7%	63.1%	64.2%	64.4%
35.	Colgate -Palmotive	54.1%	56.0%	64.4%	63.7%	66.6%	63.8%	64.2%	64.5%	68.4%
36.	FW Woolworth	41.5%	42.6%	43.3%	43.0%	43.6%	42.4%	43.0%	41.8%	40.7%
37.	Manufacturers Hanover	33.5%	32.7%	35.8%	36.1%	40.0%	-	-	-	-
38.	NCR	50.9%	54.6%	58.3%	59.0%	61.9%	-	-	-	-
39.	Allied -Signal	20.9%	19.3%	23.0%	21.8%	23.9%	24.7%	25.4%	22.0%	24.0%
40.	Kraft	28.2%	23.6%	-	-	-	-	-	-	-
41.	Banker Trust New York	49.7%	55.4%	46.8%	50.4%	56.2%	63.6%	59.0%	62.3%	50.0%
42.	American Brands	38.3%	47.0%	47.6%	46.2%	51.9%	49.0%	47.2%	44.2%	49.8%
43.	Kmart	9.3%	9.3%	10.4%	10.7%	10.2%	9.5%	8.8%	9.1%	-
44.	Motorola	30.0%	43.8%	48.1%	51.0%	54.2%	55.9%	60.3%	43.9%	43.9%

Exhibit 1.5 (Continued)

45.	Monsanto	32.6%	36.1%	37.1%	35.6%	36.8%	36.4%	36.1%	34.7%	35.0%
46.	Atlantic Richfield	15.4%	16.0%	16.4%	19.1%	21.8%	24.7%	24.6%	25.4%	17.3%
47.	GTE	14.1%	13.3%	14.7%	15.9%	16.6%	11.7%	11.9%	12.6%	12.9%
48.	Chrysler	9.3%	9.9%	11.6%	11.9%	12.2%	16.5%	14.5%	13.2%	12.6%
49.	Pan Am Corp	67.5%	67.8%	76.1%	71.9%	74.6%	-	-	-	-
50.	Merok	49.0%	50.6%	49.5%	46.8%	47.3%	46.3%	46.4%	43.7%	29.4%
51.	Pfizer	44.5%	46.1%	46.4%	45.4%	45.8%	45.2%	46.2%	46.4%	46.7%
52.	Sara Lee	24.1%	24.2%	26.0%	27.3%	28.6%	30.7%	34.2%	35.5%	37.2%
53.	Cater-pillar	25.5%	27.3%	29.7%	26.9%	27.0%	25.4%	25.3%	19.8%	22.6%
54.	Cinga	10.9%	12.9%	13.0%	14.9%	13.9%	14.3%	14.6%	15.3%	16.3%
55.	Phillips Petroleum	18.7%	15.1%	14.4%	14.8%	17.7%	18.5%	17.2%	16.0%	-
56.	Union Carbide	28.2%	30.9%	30.8%	33.7%	36.4%	-	-	-	-
57.	Gillete	60.9%	63.2%	65.1%	64.7%	67.0%	68.1%	69.2%	67.5%	68.0%
58.	Chemical New York	29.4%	24.3%	24.1%	-	-	-	-	-	
59.	HJ Heinz	36.7%	40.1%	41.8%	40.1%	37.9%	41.9%	41.5%	43.0%	42.9%
60.	Sun Co.	16.9%	16.2%	17.5%	18.15	22.9%	25.3%	23.0%	-	-
61.	TRW	25.3%	25.7%	27.6%	28.0%	31.2%	30.9%	31.7%	29.0%	30.8%

62.	Occidental Petroleum	9.5%	10.3%	7.5%	-	-	-	-	-	
63.	Unocal	19.4%	24.1%	18.7%	14.8%	-	-	-	-	-
64.	Texas Instruments	29.9%	31.5%	32.3%	31.4%	33.2%	35.1%	35.2%	37.7%	**42.4%**
65.	WR Grace	39.5%	37.9%	37.0%	34.8%	36.9%	41.1%	40.4%	-	-
66.	Allegis	15.3%	16.4%	-	-	-	-	-	-	-
67.	Warner-Lambert	43.7%	46.5%	47.9%	46.4%	47.8%	48.3%	49.7%	52.6%	**54.0%**
68.	Bristol-Myers	27.6%	32.5%	35.3%	40.1%	42.9%	38.4%	42.2%	41.1%	**41.8%**
69.	Smithkline Beckman	34.9%	38.1%	44.5%	-	-	-	-	-	-
70.	Eli Lilly	34.7%	35.9%	37.0%	36.3%	36.1%	36.7%	37.8%	38.3%	**42.5%**
71.	Dresser Industries	35.2%	37.0%	43.0%	42.4%	45.7%	43.9%	-	-	**47.8%**
72.	American Cyanamid	33.5%	37.2%	38.3%	38.6%	39.6%	38.7%	38.8%	-	-
73.	Deere	35.5%	32.5%	32.1%	26.3%	25.8%	28.1%	29.2%	27.5%	**27.2%**
74.	American Home Products	25.3%	29.7%	31.1%	29.5%	32.0%	31.1%	31.6%	31.4%	**34.1%**
75.	Security Pacific	20.7%	21.0%	21.3%	18.8%	19.1%	-	-	-	-
76.	Pepsi Co.	13.2%	17.2%	18.9%	17.9%	21.1%	22.6%	24.7%	26.8%	**28.9%**

Exhibit 1.5 (Continued)

77.	Kimberly-Clark	28.1%	33.4%	37.5%	37.7%	33.4%	32.1%	32.1%	32.7%	35.4%
78.	PPG Industries	25.5%	29.2%	30.0%	30.9%	34.3%	36.1%	35.8%	-	-
79.	Hercules	36.4%	-	-	-	-	-	-	-	-
80.	Rockwell International	9.6%	10.9%	16.4%	17.6%	19.5%	18.7%	18.5%	18.8%	24.7%
81.	Abbott Laboratories	30.9%	33.1%	34.0%	34.2%	36.5%	36.4%	37.4%	36.4%	37.1%
82.	American Standard	38.1%	44.7%	-	-	-	-	-	-	-
83.	Honeywell	21.7%	20.6%	23.0%	28.3%	31.8%	33.8%	35.5%	34.7%	36.8%
84.	McDonald's	27.5%	29.8%	33.2%	36.1%	41.7%	44.6%	47.4%	46.9%	50.1%
85.	Aluminum Co. of America	21.6%	39.6%	36.1%	31.3%	40.4%	42.3%	40.4%	-	-
86.	First Chicago	28.3%	-	-	-	-	-	-	-	-
87.	Scott Paper	28.5%	31.5%	32.7%	33.6%	34.1%	38.9%	40.0%	-	-
88.	Baxter Travenol	19.7%	19.9%	23.5%	21.9%	22.9%	22.7%	26.6%	25.9%	26.7%
89.	TransWorld Airlines	34.4%	34.2%	-	-	-	-	-	-	-
90.	Continental Corp.	18.0%	18.3%	-	-	-	-	-	-	-

91.	Quaker Oats	29.3%	29.3%	28.9%	28.8%	-	34.0%	35.5%	35.3%	-
92.	Kellogg	32.1%	34.3%	36.4%	36.8%	41.3%	41.1%	43.0%	39.9%	41.5%
93.	Bank of Boston	30.1%	38.7%	42.3%	45.5%	43.8%	43.6%	59.1%	67.1%	-
94.	Firestone	29.9%	-	-	-	-	-	-	-	-
95.	Hallibourton	29.6%	-	30.7%	30.6%	30.5%	38.8%	38.8%	39.9%	40.5%
96.	Avon Products	35.7%	44.1%	50.6%	52.2%	55.9%	58.0%	59.1%	61.1%	64.0%
97.	Merill Lynch	10.7%	11.1%	-	14.6%	-	-	-	25.0%	26.9%
98.	Control Data	30.3%	33.2%	-	-	-	-	-	-	-
99.	Henley Group	31.1%	-	-	-	-	-	-	-	-
100.	Schering-Plough	41.0%	40.9%	-	-	-	-	-	47.4%	45.2%

revenues include Texaco, Dow Chemical, Procter and Gamble, Eastman Kodak, Coca-Cola, Minn. Mining & Mfg., Unisys, Digital Equipment, Johnson and Johnson, American International Corp., CPC International, Colgate-Palmotive, Warner-Lambert, and McDonald's. By 1994, twenty firms had foreign revenues/total revenues ratios over 50 percent. These are the largest and most profitable firms in the United States, with 20 percent of them generating 50 percent or more of their revenues from foreign sales. They constitute the ideal sample to be used in this book to study the association between multinationality and firm performance.

CONCLUSIONS

There are various measures of multinationality, requiring great caution in the ranking of firms. One firm may be high on one measure and very low on another. Foreign revenues/total revenues remains by far the best measure of multinationality on both theoretical and empirical growth. The increase in the multinationality of firms demands the investigation of the potential association between multinationality and firm performance, with firm performance to be expressed by (a) firm value, (b) firm profitability, (c) prediction performance of earnings, and (d) corporate financing. They are examined in the next five chapters.

NOTES

1. Christopher Farrell, ''The Triple Revolution,'' *Business Week: Special Issue 1994 Bonus Issue on the 21st Century Capitalism* (1994): 16–25.

2. Ibid.

3. Ibid.

4. Ibid.

5. Karen Penmar, ''Frontiers Economies: Enter If You Dare,'' *Business Week: Special Issue 1994 Bonus Issue on the 21st Century Capitalism* (1994): 28.

6. Bill Javetski and William Glasgall, ''Borderless Finance: Fuel for Growth,'' *Business Week: Special Issue 1994 Bonus Issue on the 21st Century Capitalism* (1994): 40.

7. Ibid.

8. Paula Drvyh, Pete Engardio, Zachary Schiller, and Stanley Reed,

"Tearing up Today's Organization Chart," *Business Week: Special Issue 1994 Bonus Issue on the 21st Century Capitalism* (1994): 81–90.

9. Ibid., 82.

10. George Gunset, "Trade Accord Productive for Midwest Farm," *The Chicago Frilure* (August 13, 1992): 1.

11. M. Porter, *The Competitive Advantage of Nations* (New York: Free Press, 1989), 89–100.

12. Gerhard G. Muller, "Whys and Hows of International Accounting," *The Accounting Review* (April 1965): 386.

13. J. Fred Weston and Bart W. Sorge, "Multinationality and Common Stock Offering," *Journal of International Financial Management and Accounting* (Spring 1991): 2.

14. George P. Tsetsekos, "Multinationality and Common Stock Offering Dilution," *Journal of International Financial Management and Accounting* (Spring 1991): 2.

15. Ibid., 3.

16. C. Baldwin, "The Capital Factor: Competing for Capital in Global Environment," in M. Porter (Ed.), *Competition in Global Industries* (Boston: Harvard Business School Press, 1986), 184–223.

17. J. D. Daniel and L. H. Radebaugh, *International Business: Environments and Operations* (Reading, Mass.: Addison-Wesley, 1989).

18. J. C. Miller and B. Pras, "The Effect of Multinational and Export Diversification on the Profit Stability of U.S. Corporations," *Southern Economic Journal* 3 (1980): 78–79.

19. Sule M. Kim and Seung H. Kim, *Global Corporate Finance: Text and Cases,* 2nd edition (Miami, Fla.: Kolb Publishing Company, 1993), 333.

20. David K. Eiteman, A. I. Stonehill, and M. H. Moffelt, *Multinational Business Finance* (Reading, Mass.: Addison-Wesley, 1992), 436.

21. Ibid., 445.

22. J. H. Dunning, "Reappraising the Eclectic Paradigm in an Age of Alliance Capitalism," *Journal of International Business Studies* 26, no. 3 (1995): 461–492.

23. Michael Gerlach, *Alliance Capitalism: The Social Organization of Business* (Oxford, U.K.: Oxford University Press, 1992).

24. Jan Johanson and Jan-Erik Vahlne, "The Internationalization Process of the Firm," *Journal of International Business Studies* 8 (1977): 23–32.

25. Daniel Sullivan, "Measuring the Degree of Internationalization of a Firm," *Journal of International Business Studies* 25, no. 2 (1994): 325–342.

26. Raumcrid Vernon, *Sovereignty at Bay: The Multinational Spread of U.S. Enterprises* (New York: Basic Books, 1971).

27. J. M. Stofford and L. T. Welb, *Managing the Multinational Enterprise* (New York: Basic Books, 1972).

28. Howard U. Perbnutter, ''The Tortuous Evolution of the Multinational Corporation,'' *Columbia Journal of World Business* (January–February, 1969): 9–18.

29. John D. Daniel and John Bracker, ''Profit Performance: Do Foreign Operations Make a Difference?'' *Management International Review* 25 (1989): 46–56.

30. Lawrence Frauko, ''Global Corporate Competition: Who's Winning, Who's Losing, and the RxD Factor As a Reason Why,'' *Strategic Management Journal* 10 (1985): 49–74.

31. Richard E. Gaves, *Multinational Enterprise and Economic Analysis* (Cambridge, U.K.: Cambridge University Press, 1982).

32. D. Sullivan and A. Baver Schmidt, ''Common Factors Underlying Barriers to Export: A Study in the European and U.S. Paper Industry,'' *Management International Review* 23 (1989): 46–63.

33. D. Jan Epprik and B. Van Rhijri, ''The Internationalization of Dutch Industry,'' *Long Range Planning* 21 (1988): 54–60.

34. Sullivan, ''Measuring the Degree of Internationalization of a Firm,'' op. cit.

35. Ibid., 332.

36. Ibid.

37. Simcha Ronen and Oded Shenkar, ''Clustering Countries on Attitudinal Dimensions: A Review and Synthesis,'' *Academy of Management Review* 10 (1985): 435–454.

38. Sullivan, ''Measuring the Degree of Internationalization of a Firm,'' op. cit.

REFERENCES

Dunning, J. H. ''Reappraising the Eclectic Paradigm in an Age of Alliance Capitalism.'' *Journal of International Business Studies* 26, no. 3 (1995): 461–492.

Gerlach, Michael L. *Alliance Capitalism: The Social Organization of Business* (Oxford, U.K.: Oxford University Press, 1992).

Johanson, Jan, and Jan-Erik Vahlne. ''The Internationalization Process of a Firm.'' *Journal of International Business Studies* 8 (1977): 23–32.

Porter, M. *The Competitive Advantage of Nations* (New York: Free Press, 1989), 89–100.

Riahi-Belkaoui, Ahmed. *International and Multinational Accounting* (London: Academic Press, 1994).

Ronen, Sincha, and Oded Shenkar. ''Clustering Countries on Attitudinal Dimensions: A Review and Synthesis.'' *Academy of Management Review* 10 (1985): 435–454.

Sullivan, Daniel. ''Measuring the Degree of Internationalization of a Firm.'' *Journal of International Business Studies* 25, no. 2 (1994): 325–342.

APPENDIX 1.A: A SYNTHESIS OF FOREIGN DIRECT INVESTMENT THEORIES AND THEORIES OF THE MULTINATIONAL FIRM

A. L. CALVET*
University of Ottawa

Abstract. This paper first presents a taxonomy of the foreign direct investment theories following the market imperfections paradigm. It then focuses on recent developments pertaining to the theory of the multinational firm, specifically the appropriability, internalization, and diversification theories. Subsequently, the multinational phenomenon is seen as the result of an international differentiation of activities and an intrafirm integration across national borders — all this within a markets and hierarchies approach. Last, the paper points to areas for future research.

INTRODUCTION

■ It was twenty years ago that the late Stephen Hymer wrote his seminal thesis on foreign direct investment (FDI) and multinational enterprises (MNEs). Since then, the literature on these subjects has increased substantially and taken different directions, placing the multinational firm at the crossroads of many disciplines and of many debates as well.

Behind the proliferation of articles and books in this field, Hymer's theoretical contribution has remained unshaken and has led the way to further elaboration and refinement of the theory. One can hardly find a publication on FDI that does not make some reference to Hymer's work — which is highly indicative of its relevance. His early insights into the determinants of foreign direct investment have paved the way for further research, and major additions have taken place since, perhaps with increased frequency in the last five years. This renewed interest in the theory of the multinational firm (rather than foreign direct investment — a point to which this discussion shall return) results from various reasons, a major one being the parallel and growing interest in the economics of internal organization.

The time seems ripe for reviewing the work done over the last few years in the direction pursued by Hymer and for identifying recent trends likely to guide the future research in the field. Such is the purpose of this paper. Section one presents a taxonomy of the determinants of foreign direct investment derived from the market imperfections paradigm. Section two singles out recent contributions to the theory of the MNE. In section three a new theoretical framework is proposed — the markets and hierarchies approach — in an attempt to encompass the various strands of current research on the MNE. Finally, section four discusses areas for further study.

FOREIGN DIRECT INVESTMENT IN THE CONTEXT OF THE THEORY OF THE MARKET: THE MARKET IMPERFECTIONS PARADIGM

Kindleberger provided the first comprehensive survey of the various theories of foreign direct investment along the lines expressed by Hymer.[1] He approached the question of direct investment from the standpoint of the perfectly competitive model of neoclassical economics by asserting that in a world of pure competition direct investment could not exist. [Kindleberger 1969, p. 13] Indeed, when all markets operate efficiently, when there are no external economies of production or marketing, when information is costless and there are no barriers to trade or competition, international trade is the only possible form of international involvement.[2] Logically, it follows that it is the departures from the model of per-

*A. L. Calvet is Assistant Professor at the Faculty of Administration at the University of Ottawa. This paper is based upon his doctoral dissertation completed at M.I.T. in 1980.

The author is much indebted to John H. Dunning of the University of Reading for many valuable suggestions. Two anonymous referees also provided valuable comments. All responsibility for errors remains with the author.

fect competition that must provide the rationale for foreign direct investment. The first deviation had been noted by Hymer [1960/1976], who postulated that local firms have better information about the economic environment in their country than do foreign companies. According to his argument, two conditions have to be fulfilled to explain the existence of direct investment: (1) foreign firms must possess a countervailing advantage over the local firms to make such investment viable, and (2) the market for the sale of this advantage must be imperfect. It was, thus, a natural step for Kindleberger later to suggest that market imperfections were the reason for the existence of foreign direct investment. Specifically, he came up with the following taxonomy: imperfections in goods markets, imperfections in factor markets, scale economies and government-imposed disruptions. [1969, p. 14] This classification may be called the 'market imperfections paradigm.' To encompass new developments in the field of determinants of foreign investment, a somewhat different taxonomy from that of Kindleberger may be proposed to distinguish among four classes: (1) market disequilibrium hypotheses, (2) government-imposed distortions, (3) market structure imperfections, and (4) market failure imperfections. Some brief comments are in order to elucidate the meaning of these four categories.

The common feature found in all the hypotheses in group (1) will be the transitory nature of foreign direct investment. FDI is an equilibrating force among segmented markets which eventually comes to an end when equilibrium is reestablished; that is, when rates of return are equalized among countries. The unifying characteristic in group (2) will be the role played by either host or home governments in providing the incentive to invest abroad. Group (3) will include theories in which the behavior of firms deviates from that assumed under conditions of perfect competition, through their ability to influence market prices. Finally, in group (4) will be classified theories which depart from the technical assumptions behind the model of perfect markets; that is, the assumptions about production techniques and commodity properties. This last category will deal basically with those phenomena which lead to market failure, or, cases where "the decentralizing efficiency of that regime of signals, rules and built-in sanctions which defines a price-market system" will fail. [Bator 1958, p. 352]

Several factors support this classification scheme. In the first place, the order in which the categories appear corresponds roughly to the chronological order in which new explanations of the FDI phenomenon have occurred. They range from the old view of an integrated approach to foreign direct investment and portfolio capital flows among countries, to the more recent versions of FDI as a spin-off of welfare economics. [Johnson 1970] Second, most, if not all of the early literature on FDI fits into this categorization. Third, the categories are roughly in the order of increasing need for control over foreign operations. The justification for controlling foreign firms becomes, as we will see, stronger as we go from (1) to (4). Finally, note that (1), (2), and (4) are compatible with profit-maximizing behavior while (3) requires a restricted version of the maximization argument, due to the typical interdependencies of oligopolistic industries. By being less restrictive, growth or sales maximization, profit satisficing, or any other mode of behavior can be accommodated in any of the four categories.

Market Disequilibrium Hypotheses

The notion of a perfect economy and perfect competition requires the assumption that prices everywhere are adjusted to bring supply and demand into equilibrium. It may well be that because of segmentation in world markets, rates of return are not equalized internationally. In a disequilibrium context flows of FDI would take place until markets returned to stability. Instances of disequilibrium conditions that provide incentives to invest abroad are numerous. They basically apply to factor markets and foreign exchange markets.

Currency overvaluation is perhaps the most salient example of these disequilibrium hypotheses. A currency may be defined as overvalued when at the prevailing rate of exchange production costs for tradable goods in the country are, on the average, higher than in other countries. [Ragazzi 1973, p. 491] Such an occurrence creates opportunities for profit-making by holding assets in undervalued currencies with the expectation that, once the equilibrium in the foreign exchange market is reestablished, capital gains will be realized. In the meantime, there is an incentive to locate production of internationally traded commodities in countries with undervalued currencies and to purchase income-producing assets with overvalued money. The important point is that, once exchange rates return to equilibrium, the flow of FDI should stop. Even more, foreign investors should sell their foreign assets, pocket the capital gains, and return to domestic operations.

Foreign direct investment may be attracted toward areas where the average rates of profit are higher. This is basically the capital markets disequilibrium hypothesis. It implies that, for a given level of risk, rates of return on assets are not equalized internationally by portfolio capital flows, due to inefficiencies in securities markets—such as, thinness or lack of disclosure. Therefore, the only way that rates of return on real assets can be brought to equilibrium is by flows of direct investment. The process is, however, self-destructive because firms from low yield countries will invest in countries with high yields until rates of return are brought to equilibrium. Then foreign direct investment will cease.[3]

The same approach has been used with respect to labor costs. Here foreign direct investment would flow from high-labor-cost countries to low-cost countries in the pursuit of cost minimization. This hypothesis is no exception to the transitory character of the FDI phenomenon, because the demand for labor in countries where wages are low will tend to hike up labor costs, while the lack of demand in source countries will drive wages down. The result: A finite life for direct investment.

Finally, disequilibrium situations may arise in technology markets. Rates of technical and technological innovation may vary among nations, thereby placing some countries in leadership positions with respect to new products and processes. The origins of superior knowledge can be traced back to superior R & D performance or merely chance factors—such as, a breakthrough in scientific knowledge. In any event, firms in countries where technology is relatively advanced would find profitable opportunities abroad and would, therefore, have an incentive to invest overseas.

The previous review covers basically all the situations where conventional economic disequilibrium conditions can give rise to FDI flows. The reader will have recognized in these hypotheses the old view of FDI as an equilibrating capital flow. It is not necessary to state at length the well-known shortcomings of this traditional view of FDI—shortcomings uncovered in Hymer's thesis, which showed that FDI can better be understood within the realm of industrial organization.[4] Prior to examining this latter approach, let us look at governmental policies and their relation to FDI.

Government-Imposed Distortions

At the outset, it should be mentioned that government policies could conceivably be responsible for some of the disequilibrium hypotheses previously considered. Fixed exchange rates, wage policies, and policies regulating the migration of labor create unstable conditions apt to foster foreign investing. The main difference, however, between the two categories is that there appear to be no equilibrating forces which would correct the distortions imposed by governments. That is to say, in order to nullify the incentive for direct investment, all governments would have to harmonize their policies or have no policies at all.

Tariffs, other trade barriers (for example, quotas), and, it might be added, nontariff barriers (for example, regulations for imported goods) are often regarded as a major cause of direct investment. Other things being equal, an increase in trade barriers (or the expectation of their rise) may be the necessary incentive for firms to establish a subsidiary inside the protected market, rather than export to it.

Another major government-induced distortion is the levy of taxes.[5] Not surprisingly, the incentive to invest abroad can originate in differences in the tax laws governing countries. After all, firms try to maximize rates of return after taxes. If, furthermore, the parent government tax laws encourage expatriation of capital (for example, via a deferral system), the incentive will be even stronger to set up foreign operations.

Government-related disruptions can take many other forms—from price and profit regulation to antitrust laws or any other change in the institutional setting in which business operates. All these actions can be used to rationalize the expatriation of domestic firms on the grounds that they restrict their autonomy.

Suffice it to say that when foreign direct investment is viewed as a package made up of capital, technology, and other forms of knowledge, the tariff argument indicates only that the movement of goods via exports is denied or restricted. In principle, tariffs do not prevent the licensing route nor does it necessarily follow that the foreign firm will be interested in setting up a subsidiary in the protected market. (Other conditions must be present; for example, the market must be large enough to allow the firm to recover the costs of its initial foreign investment.) As for the tax argument, it applies mainly to cases where a firm is able to generate profits abroad as a result of its foreign operations, given that local firms have an inherent advantage resulting from their institutional knowledge. This leads us directly into the oligopolistic approach to FDI.

Market Structure Imperfections

The previous cases of disequilibrium hypotheses and government-induced distortions are compatible with a "relatively" competitive market structure. Market structure imperfections, on the other hand, refer to deviations from purely market-determined prices brought about by the existence of monopolistic or oligopolistic market characteristics. In this perspective, foreign direct investment becomes the outgrowth of industrial organization.

The recognition that foreign direct investment belongs to the realm of industrial organization goes back to Hymer's writings. [1960/1976] Since then, it has received much attention and has become the most popular approach to date. [See for example: Bergsten, Horst, and Moran 1978.] There are two essential characteristics which set oligopolistic industries apart from competitive ones. First, the former are industries where maximizing decisions—whether of profit or growth—are interdependent; each firm must speculate on the reactions of the few other firms in the industry. Second, barriers to entry are essential, in order to prevent a surge of competition. As one would expect, both of these features have been used extensively to explain foreign direct investment.

Not all barriers to entry lend themselves to direct expansion abroad. Leaving aside vertical foreign investments which respond to barriers of a different kind, Caves considered product differentiation in the home market as being the critical element giving rise to foreign investment. [1971, p. 270] The successful firm, producing a differentiated product, controls knowledge about servicing the domestic market that can be used at little or no cost in other national markets. This provides the motivation for investing abroad, as long as the means to protect the product exist; such as, patents and copyrights.

Other contributions to the oligopolistic feature of direct investment include models which explicitly take into account the interdependence of firms in the industry. The most publicized is, perhaps, the product life cycle hypothesis [Vernon 1966] where firms react to the threat of losing markets—as the product matures—by expanding overseas and capturing the remaining rent from the product's development. Variations on this approach include the "follow the leader" case, where the investment moves of one firm trigger similar moves by other leading firms in the industry [Knickerbocker 1974], and the "exchange of threats" hypothesis, where oligopolists imitate each other by establishing subsidiaries in each other's markets. [Graham 1974]

Despite their success, the problems associated with the industrial organization hypotheses are many and serious. For one, there is too great an emphasis placed on sellers' concentration as being a main determinant of direct investment. Ragazzi reported that the degree of industrial concentration was, in general, much higher in Europe than in the U.S. in the 50s, although the bulk of FDI was from the U.S. to Europe. [1973, p. 489] Also, whereas FDI theories derived from industrial organization may explain the advantages of home country firms, they cannot predict the country or industry patterns of foreign investment. [Aliber 1970, p. 20] Nor can they adequately explain the apparent preference for takeovers of domestic firms over de novo investment. Furthermore, in many instances, neither are the causal factors in the investment decision isolated – for example, in Knickerbocker's thesis [1974] – nor is the decision integrated with the alternative methods – exports and licensing – of exploiting the foreign firms' advantages in the host country. Recent evidence based on Japan's direct investment abroad tends to confirm some of the shortcomings of the industrial organization approach, because the Japanese experience shows a compatibility of international investment with a relatively competitive market structure at home. [Kojima 1978; Ozawa 1979]

Finally, and particularly in Caves's argument, the static concept of product differentiation is related to the notion of intangible capital in the form of knowledge, yet the two do not imply the same form of international involvement. Indeed, "licensing of domestically controlled firms would be a feasible alternative in industries with an unchanging product mix since quality changes, brand changes, etc. pose no difficulties for agreements." [Baumann 1975, p. 683] However, as will be seen in the next section, the transfer of intangible capital in the form of knowledge does pose serious problems.

Market Failure Imperfections

As was pointed out earlier, market failure imperfections are characteristics in production techniques and commodity properties which prevent a market mechanism from allocating resources efficiently. There are basically three types of imperfections which lead to market failures: (1) external effects, (2) public goods, and (3) economies of scale (decreasing cost industries). Under any one of these conditions, the duality between social efficiency and market performance ceases to exist. [Bohm 1973, p. 19]

The significance of market failures as a potential explanation of FDI was not fully realized until 1970. At that time, Johnson related foreign direct investment to the welfare economics of technological and managerial knowledge as a factor of production – a typical case of market failure. [1970, p. 36] His ideas were based upon previous work done by Arrow on the accumulation of knowledge in society. [1962] Briefly, the peculiarities of knowledge which make its markets so imperfect are (1) the lumpiness of the inventive input necessary to produce it, and (2) the high degree of spillover or externality that accompanies the inventive process. [Nordhaus 1969, p. 36]

This in turn creates problems for both the production and international transfer of knowledge. First, reasons of social efficiency would dictate that existing knowledge be made available as a free good. Hence the dilemma: how is the production of new knowledge to be motivated, if no property rights are granted? Second, the natural characteristics of knowledge would favor its transfer within a single firm, hence 'justifying' foreign direct investment over other alternatives of exploiting foreign markets. Indeed, if markets for knowledge are difficult to organize, internalization within the firm achieves two objectives: (1) to provide channels for the transfer of this knowledge at lower costs than via external modes [Teece 1976]; and, (2) to avoid or slow down dissipation of this knowledge to competitors.

Before ending this section, it would be of interest to take a historical perspective in order to identify stages in the development of FDI theories. The author's view distinguishes among three phases in past and current thinking about foreign direct investment. The first one—perhaps the best known—began when Hymer linked FDI to industrial organization (the study of market imperfections) and thereby ended a period in which FDI had been associated with a capital flow.[6] The Hymer-Kindleberger school of thought found its roots in the traditional theory of the market; it dealt with market imperfections in a partial equilibrium setting and emphasized above all the monopolistic nature of FDI. A quotation from Kindleberger's writings [1969, pp. 13–14] adds additional support to the author's assertion: "the nature of the monopolistic advantages which produce direct investment can be indicated under a variety of headings:. . . departures from perfect competition in goods markets,. . . departures from perfect competition in factor markets,. . . internal and external economies of scale,. . . government limitations on output or entry." All these aspects belong to the theory of the market.

The second discontinuity—or change in direction—originated with Harry Johnson in 1970. In his well-known article he attempted to go beyond the Hymer-Kindleberger framework by investigating the welfare implications of the international transfer of knowledge—the central theme of FDI. He thereby placed the FDI debate at a different level of discourse, as he himself wrote: "This paper will be concerned with essentially the same possibilities as other authors have noted, but it seeks to place the issues in a broader and more fundamental perspective by relating them to the welfare economics of technological and managerial knowledge as a factor of production." [1970, p. 36] In so doing, he introduced FDI to a much richer area of economics where one studies not only the damaging effects of monopolies and oligopolies on market functioning, but also the failure of markets, including their non existence—all within a global approach to the economic system and under the consideration of social efficiency. The direction taken by Johnson which attempts to place FDI in a global discussion of welfare economics has undoubtedly many advantages. Perhaps the most important one is showing how limited the monopolistic market imperfections perspective is. However, it also has a major disadvantage. Indeed, welfare economics has little to say in situations where prices are not taken as given, for then the resulting equilibrium need not be Pareto efficient. [Varian 1975, p. 234] In other words, whereas Johnson's ambitious perspective raises interesting questions (the production of knowledge, its appropriation, the effects on world's welfare, and so on), by the same token it raises more questions than economic theory can answer, at least at the present time. Hymer was already aware of this problem when he pointed out that to the extent that MNEs erode national power—that is, the effectiveness of governments' policies—they similarly prevent corrective governmental action in situations where it is necessary for achieving social efficiency. [Hymer 1970]

The third and current stage in the thinking about FDI began with authors such as McManus [1972], Buckley and Casson [1976], and Magee [1976]. Their most salient feature: an emphasis on the theory of the MNE, rather than on the theory of FDI. This certainly reflects more than a choice of words; it is a purposive decision to go beyond the view that MNEs create market imperfections. It is also a "switch in attention from the act of foreign direct investment. . . to the institution making the investment." [Dunning 1979, p. 274]

MULTINATIONAL ENTERPRISES IN THE CONTEXT OF THE THEORY OF THE FIRM

Although market imperfections still underlie much of the thinking on MNEs, there has been a distinctive shift in the theoretical literature toward developing a global theory of the multinational firm.[7] It was not by chance that at approximately the same time the economic profession showed signs of a renewed interest in the economics of internal organization, a new terminology evolved for an old area of economics—the theory of the firm.[8]

This section will examine three major contributions in the field: the appropriability theory, the internalization theory, and the diversification theory. The three bring new insights to our understanding of the multinational phenomenon.

The Appropriability Theory

The appropriability theory of the multinational corporation, best represented in Magee's work [1976, 1977], is a consolidation of the views of two main streams of thought: on the one hand, the industrial organization approach to foreign direct investment; on the other hand, the neoclassical ideas on the private appropriability of the returns from investments in information. MNEs are at the crossroad of these two streams of thought for, as Magee states, the distinctive nature of these corporations resides in their being specialists in the production of 'information' [technology]. [1976, p. 317] Valuable information is generated by MNEs at five different stages: new product discovery, product development, creation of the production function, market creation, and appropriability.

The theory then postulates that, because sophisticated technologies are less prone to be imitated, MNEs are more successful in appropriating the returns from these technologies than from simple ones. Furthermore, sophisticated information is transferred more efficiently via internal channels than by market means. These two factors taken together enable Magee to assert that there is a built-in incentive in the economic system to generate sophisticated information—to the detriment, in some cases, of users' needs; for example, those of less developed countries. To complete the theory, Magee goes on to say that production is information-saving so that, ultimately, there is a decline in the production of new information. All these considerations generate a technology cycle at the industry level; that is, young industries are those where information is being created at a fast pace, which in turn implies that the size of the firm expands because of the internalization of the information produced. As the industry matures, the amount of information being created is minimal. Thus, optimum firm size diminishes accordingly. In terms of the international expansion of the firm, the assertion that optimum firm size declines after the innovation stage suggests that, after a certain point, licensing should increase relative to direct investment.

The propensity to engage in takeover activity is also an implication of the appropriability theory. On the subject of takeovers, Magee states that "takeovers of host country production facilities and mergers of multinationals with host country firms are normal consequences of the expansion in optimum size early in an industry's technology cycle." In addition, takeovers, according to Magee, "may be aimed at slowing the depreciation of the stock of information by absorbing the most likely interlopers." [1976, p. 333] Note that two arguments are being used: one is the higher efficiency of intrafirm transfers dictating an internal solution; the other one is the monopolistic argument of the industrial organization approach to FDI.

The Internalization Theory

Imperfect markets for knowledge is the basis of Buckley and Casson's theory of the multinational enterprise. [1976] It is perhaps in their work that the notion of the multinational firm as an entity is given the most attention. The starting point of their theory is the idea that the modern business sector carries out many activities apart from the routine production of goods and services. All these activities, including marketing, R & D, and training of labor, are interdependent and are related through flows of intermediate products—mostly in the form of knowledge and expertise. [Buckley and Casson 1976, p. 33] However, intermediate product markets are difficult to organize due to their imperfections—which provide an incentive to bypass them. This results in the creation of internal markets; that is, bringing the activities which are linked by the market under common ownership and control. [Buckley and Casson 1976, p. 33] Finally, it is the internalization of markets across national boundaries which gives rise to the multinational enterprise. A few years earlier, McManus [1972] had already shown that the essence of the phenomenon of international production is not the transfer of capital but rather the international extension of managerial control over foreign subsidiaries—control which is ownership-based and through which management replaces the market as the allocator of resources.

Dunning [1977], expanding on the internalization theory, stated that the incentives to internalize activities are to avoid the disadvantages, or capitalize on the advantages, of imperfections on external (markets and public) mechanisms of resource allocation [1977, p. 402]. Therefore, not only must firms possess superior resources—as in Hymer's argument—they must also have the desire and the ability to internalize the advantages which result from their possession.

The Diversification Theory

Up to now the imperfections with which this discussion has been concerned were imperfections in markets for products and for knowledge. Financial market imperfections have not been generally in the forefront of the literature, "presumably because financial markets are deemed to be more efficient than markets for real goods and services" [Lessard 1979]. However, the evidence that has accumulated recently tends to suggest that there are imperfections in financial markets, and hence advantages for the MNE in internalizing financial transactions. In his recent review of the internal financial transfers within MNEs, Lessard [1979] pointed to sources of gains stemming from exchange control arbitrage, credit market arbitrage and equity market arbitrage. Undoubtedly the most well-publicized advantage accruing to MNEs is that which derives from equity market arbitrage, i.e., risk reduction through diversification.

Although the mechanics of diversification are well known, the application of international diversification to the MNE has not always been properly substantiated.[9] Originally the argument had been put forward by international portfolio theorists that variations in security returns across countries show less correlation than within a single country. An immediate implication is that international diversification can be used as a means of reducing the average risk faced by investors. However, there is nothing in this argument which would justify corporate international diversification, for in an integrated and perfectly competitive world capital market, individual investors can diversify their holdings at no cost. The issue which was subsequently raised in the literature concerned the existence of barriers or costs to capital transfers and the potential benefits to be derived from the indirect diversification provided by MNEs. In one of the first attempts to deal with this issue, Agmon and Lessard [1977] argued that two conditions must be satisfied before attributing the diversification motive to the MNE: (1) there must exist greater barriers or costs to portfolio capital flows than to direct investment flows; and (2) investors must recognize that MNEs provide a diversification vehicle which would otherwise not be available. More recently, Errunza and Senbet [1980], taking a more general equilibrium perspective, have been able to show, however, that the existence of barriers *per se* does not yield price differentials among purely domestic and multinational stocks. Within a framework which allows for (1) supply adjustments by MNEs, and (2) interactions of barriers to international flows faced by both firms and investors, these authors have derived conditions under which the diversification services by MNEs get "priced out" in equilibrium. In other words, in a well-functioning domestic capital market, investors must accept a smaller equilibrium expected return on multinational stocks, and hence must pay a price premium to hold those stocks. Consequently, the pricing effects of international involvement by the MNE become hard to isolate empirically.

Tests on the diversification theory of the MNE had also, in the past, suffered from serious shortcomings. Agmon and Lessard [1977] provided limited evidence that investors "recognize" the international involvement of U.S. multinationals. Jacquillat and Solnik [1978] found, however, that portfolios made up of MNEs' shares are poor substitutes for international portfolio diversification, and that the extent of foreign influence on stock prices is very limited when compared to the extent of firms' foreign involvement. The difficulty with these and other tests on the behavior of MNEs' share prices is that (1) they rely on traditional risk-return generating processes and performance evaluation techniques which cannot assess whether FDI is beneficial to investors in terms of contributing to market value, and (2) more importantly, they are carried out without a fully developed theoretical model of the pricing of risky assets in an international context.[10] The recent work of Errunza and Senbet [1980] avoids some of the shortcomings of other studies by using a value-based – rather than a price-based – method to assess the effects of international operations. Briefly, they demonstrate that (1) there existed a positive and systematic relationship between the current degree of international involvement and the excess market value of U.S. multinationals over a ten-year time span, and (2) the monopoly rents derived by these firms were stronger during the sub-period in which barriers to capital flows were in effect. That is to say, the stronger relationship between international involvement and monopoly rents during the period characterized by barriers to capital flows (as compared to a later period with no restrictions) is indicative of the benefits to be derived from financial market imperfections, over and above those to be attributed to real market imperfections.

These three new approaches to the phenomenon of international production undoubtedly represent a step forward in explaining the propensity of firms to choose the foreign direct investment route over alternative ways, such as licensing, in order to exploit foreign markets. All three theories, however, offer a double-edged view of the MNE: on the one hand, multinationals appear to take advantage of imperfections to enhance their already impressive power[11]; on the other hand, they facilitate the transfer of factors, goods, and services, transfers which would otherwise be handled inefficiently, or not at all. Future empirical work comparable to Teece's [1976] may possibly shed further light on the question of whether MNEs create, extend, and/or perpetuate market imperfections, or whether they are a vehicle for overcoming natural imperfections to the benefit of all parties.

In spite of the progress that these approaches already represent, one can elucidate further the institutionalization of international production within the MNE by combining ideas drawn from these new explanations with earlier theoretical contributions to the FDI literature.

MARKETS AND HIERARCHIES: TOWARD A THEORY OF INTERNATIONAL BUSINESS

The early emphasis in FDI literature on departures from perfect markets was consistent with the historical development of economic theorizing. Economists approached the phenomenon of international production at first with a simple neoclassical view of the world. This led one of Kindleberger's students to state: "Paradoxically, the unifying concept for analysis of direct investment has been the static, profit maximizing, perfectly competitive market model of general equilibrium, with perfect information and no transactions costs." [McClain 1975, p. 181] Such an approach has, however, limited applicability for understanding the MNE because it is too general. In fact, justifying the role of MNEs solely on the basis of market imperfections is comparable to rationalizing the need for governmental allocation policies (such as, anti-trust laws and stabilization policies) because we live in an 'imperfect' economy. In other words, welfare economists as well as economists studying the MNE refer to the same imperfections (monopoly, oligopoly, natural imperfections) in their analysis, so that the rationalization of two phenomena so apparently distant – multinational firms and government intervention in the economy – rests upon the same theoretical basis. Upon reflection, this is no mere coincidence. What the market imperfections paradigm indicates is simply that firms and governments are substitutes for market allocations.

The efforts of Buckley and Casson [1976], Magee [1976], and Dunning [1977], discussed earlier, have gone in the direction of both negating some of the narrow assumptions of the early neoclassical approach and concentrating on the institution making the investment. Building upon these contributions, this section will elaborate further on a particular assumption of the neoclassical model which has come under renewed criticism[12] recently and the removal of which is crucial to understanding organizations: the assumption of zero transactions costs when operating a market. To see clearly the relevance of this assumption to international business a short digression is necessary.

Hardly anyone would deny that cooperative action is a necessity and that it involves interdependence between individuals. The necessary interdependence of individuals that underlies any productive activity calls for transactions or exchanges in which agents who supply capital, those who supply labor, and those who bring their expertise, and so on, receive something of value in return. Recognition of such basic facts makes the study of the various means by which these multiple transactions are organized an issue worth exploring. An investigation of the different modes of transacting becomes a central question for economics, to the extent that the interest resides in the efficiency with which transactions are carried out between individuals.

Economic theory showed long ago that competitive markets exhibit superior coordinating properties for the organization of economic exchanges. Specifically, provided that some important assumptions are met[13] (in particular, no transactional frictions), the allocation of resources which results under a system of competitive markets is Pareto optimal.

While providing a very powerful reason for justifying the organization of transactions through the mechanism of competitive markets, economic theory left itself exposed to a question first raised by Coase [1937] and since then taken up again by Malmgren [1961]: "why do multi-person, multi-process firms exist in a competitive economy?" and he went on to add: "to say that firms exist because co-ordination of production is required is to miss the point entirely. What has to be explained is why firms, in the form of willful entrepreneurs, organize production in areas where the market could do so also." [1961, pp. 400–401]

The answer to that question rests on the realization that the optimality of competitive markets in a Paretian sense does not necessarily hold true if there are non-negligible costs in using the markets. Transactions (enforcement) costs arise principally when (1) strategic or opportunistic behavior is present among agents to an exchange[14]; (2) the commodities or services traded are ambiguously defined; and (3) contractual obligations extend in time. In the typical cases where individuals are deprived of strategic behaviors (such as, shirking, gaming, cheating, or malingering) and exchange well-defined goods or services in discrete transactions, the superiority of the price mechanism may be irrefutable. However, insofar as transactions are allowed to be extended over time and refer to ambiguously defined commodities and services, and strategic behavior is allowed to be played out, enforcement and monitoring costs may become prohibitive. There is a broad consensus in the internal organization literature that, under these latter conditions, firms tend to substitute for markets, on the basis that the firms' internal control procedures are then better suited to organize transactions. [Williamson 1975]

These brief considerations, based mainly upon the work of Coase [1937] and Williamson [1975], lead to the main feature of their approach—that of treating markets on the one hand, and firms (hierarchies) on the other, as alternative modes of organizing production.[15] A much less emphasized outcome of this discussion, albeit by no means less important, is that the substitution of a hierarchy or bureaucracy for a market situation entails a profound change in the structure of interpersonal interactions and in the way in which economic exchange proceeds. In pure markets, transactions among individuals or groups are carried out at arm's length: participants share no relationships other than the ones required by the transactions themselves and can affect each other only via the market and the price system. In hierarchies, transactions take place among individuals or groups that are linked via an authority relation. (When companies are involved, the authority relation gets its legitimacy from ownership rights.) When seen in their purest forms, and from the standpoint of the degree of personal interaction required to accomplish the exchange, markets and firms can be considered as two extreme modes of organizing economic transactions. (Needless to say, many exchanges fall somewhere in between these two modes.[16] These purest cases are nevertheless interesting, because they constitute powerful categories for theorizing.)

Returning now to the subject of international production, the question of the particular form of involvement by firms outside their national boundaries can be put into a markets and hierarchies framework: why would a firm prefer to establish hierarchical links abroad rather than contract at arm's length? Stated differently, what advantages do firms find in hierarchical structures which make the latter preferable to the outright sale or license of proprietary assets to foreign-owned firms?

Phrasing the old licensing vs. direct investment question in this way is more than a semantical rearrangement of terms. First, it allows scholars who have worked on the MNE in a parallel fashion to economists, such as organizational theorists, to realize that organizations and markets are the two principal mechanisms for mediating transactions, and that organizations may be considered as examples of market failures. Therefore, our knowledge of organizations can be called upon to help us understand the reasons for their superiority in certain situations and thus complement our knowledge about markets. Second, by not assuming the primacy of one organizational mode over the other, the door is open to the investigation of the relative merits of each mode for a given environment and the kind of transaction involved. By merits are meant not only the efficiency of accomplishing the exchange but also the very fact that the transaction takes place and how it does so. This is a significant departure from economic theory which, in general, assigns an unjustified advantage to markets.

Firms do not expand abroad, though, simply because they can internalize transactions within their hierarchy. Their desire to operate internationally has to stem from other reasons too. Therefore, one must combine the hierarchies vs. markets paradigm with existing FDI hypotheses to arrive at a synthesis of the determinants of direct investment; thus, two facets of the foreign expansion of firms have to be explained. One is the foreign involvement—the multinational character; the other, the internalization within a single entity. In other words, certain factors must account for the differentiation of operations across national boundaries; other factors must explain the integration of operations within a hierarchical mode of economic organization.[17] The specification of these two sets of factors, as well as their interplay, is the subject of the remainder of this section.

International Differentiation of Operations

Foreign involvement may occur for two basic reasons: (1) the firm possesses some valuable asset which it can use in other national jurisdictions; and (2) the host country owns resources attractive to the foreign firm. This can be restated by saying that there are firm- and country-specific factors to account for a firm's foreign involvement. A similar terminology was used by Dunning [1977; 1979] when he called the firm's internal factors 'ownership-specific endowments,' and its external factors 'location-specific endowments.' Location-specific factors refer not only to the endowments of countries, but also to gains arising from the geographical positioning of multiplant operations.[18]

Ownership-specific endowments have long been recognized as relevant to an understanding of foreign direct investment. The possession of proprietary intangible assets, such as technological expertise or entrepreneurial skills, confers to their owners the oft-cited advantage that foreign firms have over local enterprises. This is the crux of the industrial organization approach. The reason why certain firms should possess intangible assets not easily acquired by other firms, be they domestic or foreign, is not at all clear [Graham 1974, p. 85], although in a recent paper Dunning [1979] attributes them to country-specific factors. In any event, it gives rise to monopolistic power (as argued by Hymer [1960]) to be exploited abroad.

Akin to the 'superior' knowledge argument is the idea that monopolistic power arises in part from the property rights granted to firms to protect their assets and is translated into high rates of return on invested capital. To the extent that knowledge can be considered a public good, the property rights theory is undoubtedly relevant in explaining partially the monopolistic advantage that some firms have and indirectly the potential foreign involvement of a firm.

In short, the theories of industrial organization and of property rights must be considered when seeking explanations for the international involvement of firms. However, they both neglect the fact that production and distribution take place in geographical space where time, distance, and environmental differences are also of primary importance. The location-specific factors complement the firm-specific ones by adding the multinationality dimension—ignored by the latter. In this case, foreign involvement results from the advantages inherent in different geographical locations. In turn, the advantages to be gained are of two sorts: (1) those stemming from comparative cost as analyzed in international trade theory; and (2) those accruing to multiplant firms by means of multiplant economies. Hence, abundance of skilled labor, easy access to energy sources, cheap sources of capital, or protected markets—all these elements contribute to making a specific country attractive to foreign manufacturers. Also, multiplant economies give advantages to firms which locate in various countries, as shown recently by Scherer et al. [1975].

In summary, the author agrees with FDI literature that the theory of industrial organization, the theory of property rights, and the location theory are all related to the foreign involvement of firms. But nothing in these theories as yet shows that the involvement must be one of ownership control.

Intrafirm Integration of Foreign Operations

The choice of the mode of transacting (markets and hierarchies being the extreme forms) is a subsequent step in the international expansion of the firm. Hierarchical links must be weighed against other alternatives for servicing foreign markets, such as exporting, licensing, and joint-venturing. To illustrate the fact that the choice of a transacting mode obeys different rules from those which justify foreign involvement, consider the diversification theory as applied to FDI. This theory can be put to good use by showing the fallacy of many explanations of FDI. It has been argued that a firm diversifying its activities and assets internationally reduces the variance of its earnings, to the extent that cycles in various countries are not perfectly correlated. Assuming that firms are keen to diversify internationally, this strategy does not necessarily imply direct control.[19] One could imagine two or more firms from different countries doing so by means of a contract, which would stipulate a share of total earnings for each firm. In other words, suppose a firm from the U.S. locates a suitable partner in Britain, another one in Japan, and one more in West Germany willing to pool their earnings and divide the total according to a predetermined share. In so doing, fluctuations will be smoothed and the benefits of international diversification of the firm's operations reaped without the need to invest abroad. In pursuing this imaginary situation, one can easily see the kinds of problems which will be faced by the partners to such a deal: disagreements will arise as to the respective shares, the level of profits contributed by each partner, the enforcement of contract clauses, and other matters. The lack of control that each firm has over the activities of the others represents the sensitive issue in this imaginary situation. Moreover, one can identify more readily the role a hierarchy plays if one notices that the diversification that has been discussed is of a passive type: no attempts are made to alter the distribution of earnings (cash flows) in the example, only to reduce their average risk. The second facet of the diversification strategy is an active one, where a MNE tries to change the distribution of cash flows by modifying the real activities within the firm (that is, among subsidiaries and the parent firm).[20] The autonomy and flexibility with which a hierarchy can implement these changes cannot be attributed to a contractual, market-like agreement. No doubt, although hierarchical links may not be important for diversification, they are necessary for international risk alteration. To reiterate an argument stated earlier: the diversification motive is a reason for desiring foreign involvement, but it is not a sufficient reason for deciding on the mode of transacting. These are two separate issues.

In short, albeit firm- and location-specific factors determine the willingness of the firm to engage in foreign operations, the choice of the mode of transacting obeys institutional or organizational considerations. Here, internalization means the substitution of hierarchical relations for contractual modes.

An Eclectic Framework for the Multinational Phenomenon

The preceding discussion points to the rise of the multinational firm as the resultant of several forces that no single theory can encompass. Baumann [1975] clearly recognized the need for an eclectic approach, and Dunning unambiguously embraced the same position. In the latter's words: "In presenting the systemic theory [of ownership advantages], we accept we are in danger of being accused of eclectic taxonomy." [1977, p. 406] As shown earlier, an eclectic approach implies that location theory, industrial organization theory, and property rights theory all have something to contribute to an explanation of why firms decide to transact with foreign countries. To these must be added a hierarchies vs. markets theory, to account for the choice of mode of transacting. One could then argue that the international involvement of firms is best accounted for by: (1) location theory; (2) industrial organization theory; and, (3) property rights theory. For example, the higher the cost differentials between countries, the higher the advantages to be gained from multiple locations in different countries; the more R & D or advertising expenditures, the stronger the patent protection or the monopolistic returns of firms, the more important the degree of multinationalism would be.[21] In turn, the establishment of a multinational hierarchy is best accounted for by the markets and hierarchies theory, as was shown earlier.

Most common explanations for the existence of MNEs found in the FDI literature take for granted that markets are prevented from functioning efficiently—by monopolistic power, for instance. Hence, no institutional choice is necessary, for the domestic configuration of market power determines the international mode of transacting. In other words, industrial organization theory is a reason for both the international differentiation and the internal integration of the firm's activities.

The author's approach differs in that he is not satisfied with using the same arguments to explain multinationalism and the rise of multinational hierarchies. To arrive at a satisfactory answer, it has been assumed that transaction costs are ubiquitous and that their existence gives rise to a decision process regarding the appropriate institutional vehicle to transact internationally. It is therefore not obvious a priori which means of transacting will likely ensue, without specifying the nature of the transaction and the environment in which it will take place. Some transactions may best be handled by markets, others by hierarchies – in particular, when markets fail; that is, when they do not exist or are too costly to use. In so doing, the approach does not deny that certain firms may well 'create' market imperfections. But it is suggested that, by and large, it is the limitations of markets per se which enable us to understand the emergence of hierarchies in general and multinational hierarchies in particular. And these limitations have their roots in organizational factors. Briefly, the markets and hierarchies paradigm suggests that the technological determinism of FDI and MNE theories be replaced by one that is based upon transactional considerations where human and organizational behaviors play a central role.

FUTURE RESEARCH IN INTERNATIONAL BUSINESS

Putting into perspective the previous discussion, it is clear that the trend is toward investigating the nature of MNEs; that is, the reasons for their existence. It is also obvious that, although MNEs' operating modes are different, research on MNEs has to parallel research being made on the theory of the firm, at large.

Furthermore, the abandonment of the strict neoclassical framework, which assigns an undue advantage to the study of markets, enables one to investigate conditions – both at the environmental and organizational levels – which would favor either the establishment of markets or of hierarchies. Moreover, interfirm and intrafirm behaviors must be compared to ascertain some of their commonalities (for example, the use of shadow prices within firms) and their differences. More specifically, an interesting area of research is the investigation of the sharing of transactions between firms and markets, across industries, countries, and over time.

It should be noted that the markets and hierarchies framework, while being a powerful paradigm for discussing alternative modes of mediating transactions, is of a static nature.[22] More needs to be said about the forces which move economic transactions to be internalized or externalized. Only then would we be in a position to ascertain when MNEs create market imperfections and when they respond to them. Failure to develop the dynamic side of the paradigm would lead us to the dangerous road where all hierarchical or bureaucratical forms are de facto efficient responses to market failures. This need not be the case.

Behavioral issues within MNEs are also an area for further research. Managerial policies are indeed crucial for the successful operation of these large organizations, because they establish the control relationship on which the existence of a firm rests. And, the expansion of MNEs via acquisition activity deserves further study because it raises interesting questions concerning the valuation of assets in an international context.

The future of international business cannot be dissociated from an investigation of the possible arrangements of transacting internationally which fall between these two extreme forms – markets and hierarchies. Nor can it be cut off from much larger issues that have been carefully and purposely avoided, such as the political and social implications of the spread of hierarchical forms internationally. Finally, the future of international business cannot be understood without an awareness of changing trends in the sharing of decision making among the various groups in society and primarily within domestic hierarchies. For these changes cannot but affect the way international business will be conducted years hence.

FOOTNOTES

1. Several other surveys of the FDI literature appeared in the early and mid seventies discussing the respective merits of the various streams of economic theory (capital, trade, location, and investment theories) in explaining the phenomenon of international production. See for instance Ragazzi [1973], Dunning [1973], Stevens [1974], and Hufbauer [1975].

2. This assertion follows from the Heckscher-Ohlin theory of international trade. Trade of goods will equalize factor prices in a world of factor immobility. See Dunning [1977] for a discussion of this point.

3. Hufbauer [1975] provides a good criticism of this hypothesis, sometimes called 'the differential-return hypothesis.'

4. Most surveys have uncovered the many shortcomings of this approach to FDI and it is not necessary to repeat these well-known criticisms. The interested reader may refer to Dunning [1973; 1977; 1979].

5. See the work by Horst [1971; 1977; 1978].

6. The inappropriateness of international capital theory in explaining foreign direct investment comes from its ignorance of the composite nature of the international transfer of resources and the channels through which it takes place.

7. Recent attempts include those of Buckley and Casson [1976], Casson [1979], Hood and Young [1979], and Rugman [1979].

8. See for instance the Special Issues on the Economics of Internal Organization, *Bell Journal of Economics*, Spring and Autumn 1975.

9. Prachowny [1972] and Stevens [1972] concentrate on the risk-reducing benefits of diversification without explaining why these are uniquely realized through the MNE. See Lessard [1979] for a criticism of these approaches. Rugman [1975] emphasizes the higher stability of earnings achieved by MNEs, an argument which also conflicts with the 'homemade diversification theorem' which shows that firms need not diversify for individuals.

10. The interested reader may refer to Adler's comments [1980] and the reply by Agmon and Lessard [1980]. Also, a criticism of the two-factor world market model to assess the impact of foreign involvement is contained in Errunza and Yalovsky [1978].

11. Logically, a policy recommendation for MNEs is that they should scan the world environment in search of 'profitable' imperfections.

12. See McManus [1975] and Williamson [1975].

13. Economics does not have an immutable set of assumptions nor an indisputable definition for all concepts used when deriving the theorem about the optimality of a system of competitive markets in allocating scarce resources. Roughly, certain assumptions must be made about the technology, the availability of information, the characteristics of goods and services and the absence of monopoly power to prove that there exists a set of market prices such that profit-maximizing firms and utility-maximizing consumers who respond to these prices will automatically cause the economy to attain a Pareto optimal position. See Davis and Kamien [1969].

14. The concept of strategic behavior extends the considerations of self-seeking interest found in economics to encompass "false or empty, that is, self-disbelieved, threats and promises in the expectation that individual advantage will thereby be realized." [Goffman 1969, p. 105]

15. A good review of Williamson's approach within the context of other recent approaches to economic theorizing is Marris and Mueller [1980].

16. This point is developed in Calvet [1980].

17. This distinction is similar to that of Niehans [1977].

18. See on this subject Scherer et al. [1975].

19. The author also assumes that capital markets cannot be used by individual investors, so that the 'homemade diversification theorem' does not apply.

20. The author is indebted to Donald Lessard for this argument.

21. Multinationalism is here synonymous with international involvement.

22. The author owes this point to an anonymous referee.

REFERENCES

Adler, M. "Comment on: Agmon, T. and D. R. Lessard, Investor Recognition of Corporate International Diversification," 1980. (Forthcoming in *Journal of Finance.*)

Agmon, T. B., and Lessard, D. R. "Investor Recognition of Corporate International Diversification." *Journal of Finance*, September 1977, pp. 1049–1055.

Agmon, T. B., and Lessard, D. R. "Investor Recognition of Corporate International Diversification: Reply." 1980. (Forthcoming in *Journal of Finance.*)

Aho, C. M. "Foreign Direct Investment: Theories and Empirical Evidence." Manuscript of a paper written for the Council on International Economic Policy, 1974.

Aliber, R. Z. "A theory of Direct Foreign Investment." In *The International Corporation*, edited by C. P. Kindleberger. Cambridge, MA: MIT Press, 1970.

Arrow, K. J. "Economic Welfare and the Allocation of Resources for Invention." In *The Rate and Direction of Inventive Activity: Economic and Social Factors*, National Bureau of Economic Research. Princeton: Princeton University Press, 1962.

Bator, F. M. "The Anatomy of Market Failure." *Quarterly Journal of Economics*, August 1958, pp. 351-379.

Baumann, J. G. "Merger Theory, Property Rights and the Pattern of U. S. Direct Investment in Canada." *Weltwirtschaftliches Archiv* 7 (1975), pp. 676-698.

Bergsten, C. F.; Horst, T.; and Moran, T. H. *American Multinationals and American Interests*. Washington, DC: The Brookings Institution, 1978.

Bohm, P. *Social Efficiency: A Concise Introduction to Welfare Economics*. New York: John Wiley & Sons, 1973.

Buckley, P. J., and Casson, M. C. *The Future of the Multinational Enterprise*. London: The MacMillan Press, 1976.

Calvet, A. L. "Markets and Hierarchies: Towards a Theory of International Business." Doctoral dissertation, Sloan School of Management, M.I.T., 1980.

Casson, M. C. *Alternatives to the Multinational Enterprise*. London: MacMillan, 1979.

Caves, R. E. "International Corporations: The Industrial Economics of Foreign Investment." *Economica*, February 1971, pp. 1-27.

Coase, R. H. "The Nature of the Firm." *Economica*, November 1937, pp. 386-405.

Davis, O. A., and Kamien, M. I. "Externalities, Information and Alternative Collective Action." *The Analysis and Evaluation of Public Expenditure: The PPB System*. Joint Economic Committee, 91st Cong., 1st Session, 1969.

Dunning, J. H. "The Determinants of International Production." *Oxford Economic Papers*, November 1973, pp. 289-336.

________. "Trade, Location of Economic Activity and the MNE: A Search for an Eclectic Approach." In *The International Allocation of Economic Activity*, edited by B. Ohlin, P. O. Hesselborn, and P. M. Wijkman. New York: Holmes and Meier Publishers Inc., 1977.

________. "Explaining Changing Patterns of International Production: In Defence of the Eclectic Theory." *Oxford Bulletin of Economics and Statistics*, November 1979, pp. 269-295.

Errunza, V. R., and Yalovsky, M. "International Diversification and the Multinational Corporation." Working Paper, McGill University, Montreal, 1978.

Errunza, V. R., and Senbet, L. W. "The Effects of International Operations on the Market Value of the Firm: Theory and Evidence." Unpublished manuscript, September 1980. (Forthcoming in *Journal of Finance*.)

Goffman, I. *Strategic Interaction*. Philadelphia: University of Pennsylvania Press, 1969.

Graham, E. M. *Oligopolistic Imitation and European Direct Investment in the United States*. Doctoral dissertation, Harvard Business School, 1974.

Hood, N., and Young, S. *The Economics of Multinational Enterprise*. London: Longman, 1979

Horst, T. O., "The Theory of the Multinational Firm: Optimal Behavior Under Different Tariff and Tax Rates." *Journal of Political Economy*, September/October 1971, pp. 1059-1072.

________. "American Taxation of Multinational Corporations." *American Economic Review*, June 1977, pp. 376-389.

________. "Tax Issues." In *American Multinationals and American Interests*, edited by C. F. Bergsten, T. O. Horst, and T. H. Moran. Washington, DC: The Brookings Institution, 1978, Chapter 6.

Hufbauer, G. C. "The Multinational Corporation and Direct Investment." In *International Trade and Finance*, edited by P. B. Kenen. Cambridge: Cambridge University Press, 1975.

Hymer, S. H. *The International Operations of National Firms: A Study of Direct Foreign Investment*. Cambridge, MA: MIT Press, 1976.

________. "The Efficiency (Contradictions) of Multinational Corporations." *American Economic Review*, May 1970, pp. 441-448.

Jacquillat, B., and Solnik, B. "Multinationals are Poor Tools for Diversification." *The Journal of Portfolio Management*, Winter 1978, pp. 8-12.

Johnson, H. G. "The Efficiency and Welfare Implications of The International Corporation." In *The International Corporation*, edited by C. P. Kindleberger. Cambridge, MA: MIT Press, 1970

Kindleberger, C. P. *American Business Abroad: Six Lectures on Direct Investment*. New Haven: Yale University Press, 1969.

Knickerbocker, F. T. *Oligopolistic Reaction and Multinational Enterprise*. Cambridge, MA: Harvard Business School Division of Research, 1974.

Kojima, K. *Direct Foreign Investment: A Japanese Model of Multinational Business Operations*. London: Groom Helm, 1978.

Lessard, D. R. "Transfer Prices, Taxes and Financial Markets: Implications of Internal Financial Transfers within the Multinational Firm." In *Economic Issues of Multinational Firms*, edited by R. G. Hawkins. Greenwich, CT: JAI Press, 1979.

Magee, S. P. "Technology and the Appropriability Theory of the Multinational Corporation." In *The New International Economic Order*, edited by Jagdish Bhajwati. Cambridge MA: MIT Press, 1976.

________. "Multinational Corporations, the Industry Technology Cycle and Development." *Journal of World Trade Law*, July/August 1977, pp. 297-321.

Malmgren, H. "Information, Expectations and the Theory of the Firm." *Quarterly Journal of Economics*, August 1961, pp. 399-421.

Marris, R., and Mueller, D. C. "The Corporation, Competition, and the Invisible Hand." *Journal of Economic Literature*, March 1980, pp. 32-63.

McClain, D. "The Determinants of Foreign Direct Investment in the U.S." Ph.D. Thesis, Department of Economics, M.I.T., 1975.

McManus, J. C. "The Theory of the International Firm." In *The Multinational Firm and the Nation State*, edited by C. Paquet. Toronto: Collier-Macmillan, 1972.

________. "The Costs of Alternative Economic Organizations." *Canadian Journal of Economics*, August 1975, pp. 334-350.

Niehans, J. "Benefits of Multinational Firms for a Small Parent Economy: The Case of Switzerland." In *Multinationals from Small Countries*, edited by T. Agmon and C. P. Kindleberger. Cambridge, MA: MIT Press, 1977.

Nordhaus, W. D. *Invention, Growth, and Welfare*. Cambridge, MA: MIT Press, 1969.

Ozawa, T. "International Investment and Industrial Structure: New Theoretical Implications from the Japanese Experience." *Oxford Economic Papers*, March 1979, pp. 72-92.

Prachowny, M. F. J. "Direct Investment and the Balance of Payments of the United States: A Portfolio Approach." In *International Mobility and Movement of Capital*, edited by F. Machlup, et al. New York: Columbia University Press, 1972.

Ragazzi, G. "Theories of the Determinants of Direct Foreign Investment." *IMF Staff Papers*, July 1973, pp. 471-498.

Rugman, A. M. "Motives for Foreign Investment: The Market Imperfections and Risk Diversification Hypotheses." *Journal of World Trade Law*, September/October 1975, pp. 567-573.

________. *International Diversification and the Multinational Enterprise*. Lexington, MA: Lexington Books, 1979.

Scherer, F. M.; Beckenstein, A. R.; Kaufer, E.; and Murphy, R. D. *The Economics of Multiplant Operation: An International Comparisons Study*. Cambridge, MA: Harvard University Press, 1975.

Stevens, G. V. "Capital Mobility and the International Firm." In *The International Mobility and Movement of Capital*, edited by F. Machlup, et al. New York, Columbia University Press, 1972.

________. "Determinants of Investment." In *Economic Analysis and the Multinational Enterprise*, edited by J. H. Dunning. London; Allen & Unwin, 1974.

Teece, D. J. *The Multinational Corporation and the Resource Cost of International Technology Transfer*. Cambridge, MA: Ballinger, 1976.

Varian, H. R. "Distributive Justice, Welfare Economics, and the Theory of Fairness." *Philosophy & Public Affairs* 4 (1975), pp. 223-247.

Vernon, R. "International Investment and International Trade in the Product Cycle." *Quarterly Journal of Economics*, May 1966, pp. 190-207.

Williamson, O. E. *Markets and Hierarchies: Analysis and Antitrust Implications*. New York: Free Press, 1975.

Source: A. L. Calvet, ''A Synthesis of Foreign Direct Investment Theories and Theories of the Multinational Firm,'' *Journal of International Business Studies* (Spring/Summer 1981): 43–59. Reprinted with permission.

2

Multinationality, Profitability, and Firm Value

INTRODUCTION

Financial statements can be viewed as providing both earnings and nonearnings information. The nonearnings information refers to all data items reported in annual financial statements other than earnings, including earnings components.[1]

Various studies showed the ability of nonearnings accounting variables to predict future earnings changes and information content.[2] The nonearnings variables examined were mostly descriptors that have been directly or indirectly tested in prior incremental information content studies under different approaches. This chapter adds to this literature. More specifically, we focus on a nonearnings variable, multinationality, and examine its role in the prediction of future profitability and firm valuation. Multinationality refers to the degree of internationalization (DOI) of a firm's operations in terms of sales or production. Multinationality is chosen as a target of investigation for the following reasons. First, it has not been examined in previous research. Second, various authors praised its role in the profitability and valuation of multinational firms.[3]

This study relies on Ohlson's[4,5] valuation model to explain how productivity affects firm value. Penman[6] and Bernard[7] relied on the same model to show that book value and future return on equity (ROE) are key components in the accounting valuation model. Using this framework, we first examine the impact of multinationality on future ROE, and then investigate whether multinationality explains cross-sectional differences in market value incremental to those explained by book value and current ROE.

The results of this chapter indicate that multinationality does not provide much information about future profitability incremental to that provided by current profit rate, but explains cross-sectional differences in market value incremental to that explained by book value and current profit rate.

MULTINATIONALITY AND PREDICTION

This study examines multinationality as a predictor of future profitability and firm valuation.

First, the predictive ability of multinationality in the context of profitability is an open research question in the international accounting and business literature. However, studies examining the direction of the relation between the degree of internationalization and the financial performance of a firm reported either a positive, indeterminate, or negative relation. The different results have been attributed to the diversity in the choice of measures of multinationality and past or present financial performance. This study argues that the results may be due to the failure to connect multinationality to future financial performance.

Second, whether investors recognize the enhancement of firm value through internationalization is also an open research question. Both conceptual and empirical research argue for a positive relation between multinationality and firm value. Conceptually, the multinational corporation is a collection of valuable options and generates arbitrage profits that enhance its value. Empirically, there is evidence indicating that multinational firms show lower systematic risk and unsystematic risk compared to securities of purely domestic firms. Both conceptual and empirical findings indicate that the pricing of securities includes a consideration of the degree of internationalization as an unbooked or hidden asset.

TEST MODELS

Multinationality and the Prediction of Future Profitability

This chapter uses current ROE as a benchmark explanatory variable in the prediction of future profitability and adds productivity as an additional variable.

$$\textit{Model 1:}\quad \mathrm{ROE}_{it+1} = B_0 + B_1\mathrm{ROE}_{it} + e_{it}, \qquad (1)$$

where

$$\mathrm{ROE}_{it+1} = \frac{X_{t+1}}{\mathrm{BV}_{t0}}$$

X_{t+1} = Net income for year $t + 1$,

BV_{t0} = Book value of common equity at the end of year t.

Model 1 is used as a first step to examine the role of current ROE in predicting future ROE. The second step is to incorporate productivity in the model and evaluate the incremental information it provides.

$$\textit{Model 2:}\quad \mathrm{ROE}_{it+1} = B_0 + B_1\mathrm{ROE}_{it} + B_2\mathrm{DOI} + e_{it}, \qquad (2)$$

where

DOI = Degree of internationalization measured by foreign revenues/total revenues

Multinationality and the Value of the Firm

The model can be used to explain cross-sectional differences in market value on the basis of accounting numbers.

A valuation equation is used to develop test models that examine the valuation implications of productivity within an accounting framework.

$$MV_t = BV_t + \sum_{\tau=1}^{\infty} \rho - \tau\, E_t\, [X^a_{t+\tau}], \qquad (3)$$

where

MV_t = Market value of the firm at the end of year t,
BV_t = Book value of the firm at the end of year t,
ρ = One plus risk-free rate,
X^a_t = Abnormal earnings = $X_t - (\rho - 1)\, BV_{t-1}$,
X_t = Accounting earnings.

Assuming that abnormal earnings follow an AR(1) process, we can rewrite equation (3) as follows:

$$MV_t = BV_t + \psi\, E_t\, [X^a_{t+1}], \qquad (4)$$

where

$\psi = \sum_{\tau=1}^{\infty} \rho^{-\tau}\phi^{\tau-1}$,
ϕ = AR(1) parameter.

By replacing X^a_{t+1} with $X_{t+1} - (\rho - 1)BV_t$, we get

$$MV_t = BV_t + \psi\, E_t[X_{t+1} - (\rho - 1)BV_t]. \qquad (5)$$

Since $ROE_{t+1} = \frac{X_{t+1}}{BV_t}$, we can rewrite equation (5) in terms of ROE:

$$MV_t = \psi\, (1 - \rho + \frac{1}{\psi} + E_t[ROE_{t+1}])\, BV_t. \qquad (6)$$

By substituting $E_t[ROE_{t+1}]$ with current accounting variables, as proposed by model 2 described in the previous section, we can express market value as a function of current accounting variables:

$$MV_t = \psi\, (1 - \rho + \frac{1}{\psi} + \beta_o + \beta_1 ROE_t + \beta_2 DOI_t)\, BV_t. \qquad (7)$$

From equation (5), we develop the following test models:

Model 3: $MV_{it} = \gamma_0 + \gamma_1 BV_{it} + e_{it},$ (8)

Model 4: $MV_{it} = \gamma_0 + (\gamma_1 + \gamma_2 ROE_{it})BV_{it} + e_{it},$ (9)

Model 5: $MV_{it} = \gamma_0 + (\gamma_1 + \gamma_2 ROE_{it} + \gamma_3 DOI_{it})$
$BV_{it} + e_{it},$ (10)

where

MV_{it} = Market value of common equity per share for firm *i* at the end of year *t*,
BV_{it} = Book value of common equity per share for firm *i* at the end of year *t*,
DOI = Degree of internationalization measures by foreign revenues/total revenues.

SAMPLE SELECTION AND DESCRIPTIVE STATISTICS

Since 1979, *Forbes* has annually ranked the "most international" 100 manufacturing and service firms on the basis of total revenues. All the firms in *Forbes*'s classification from 1987 to 1992 were also included in our sample, resulting in 544 firm-year observations. The measure of DOI—foreign revenues/total revenues (FRTR)—is obtained from the Compustat Annual Primary-Secondary-Tertiary database. Sample descriptive statistics are presented in Exhibit 2.1.

TEST RESULTS

Results on Future Profitability

Exhibit 2.2 shows the results on multinationality and profitability. Panel A shows, as reported for other studies, that current ROE provides information about future ROE in all the years examined. However, with the exception of the results for 1987–1989, Panel B shows that multinationality, as measured by FRTR, does not continually provide information about a firm's profitability that is incremental to that provided by current profitability.

Exhibit 2.1
Descriptive Statistics

Variables	Mean	Standard Deviation
ROE_t	0.1908	0.2386
ROE_{t+1}	0.2072	0.3037
FRTR	37.4525	15.8514
Equity	$4997.199	6553.81
Market Value	$10433.05	12456.31

Results on Market Value

Exhibit 2.3 shows the results on multinationality and firm value. Panel A shows, as expected from other studies, that book value is related to the market value of equity for all years examined. Panel B shows that current profitability provides information about market value that is incremental to that provided by the book value of equity. The R^2 increased for each of the years examined. Panel C shows the incremental explanatory power of multinationality as evidenced by the increase in R^2 from model 4 to model 5 for the six years examined.

SUMMARY AND CONCLUSIONS

The study investigates the role of multinationality in the prediction of future profitability and firm valuation. The results indicate that multinationality as measured by foreign revenues over total revenues does not provide much information about future profitability incremental to that provided by current profit rate, but explains cross-sectional differences in market value incremental to that explained by book value and current profit rate. The study shows that multinationality is useful in understanding the role of accounting variables in the prediction of firm valuation.

Exhibit 2.2
Multinationality and Profitability

Panel A
Model 1: $ROE_{it+1} = B_0 + B_1 ROE_{it} + e_{it}$

Year	Number of Firms	B_0[i]	B_1	R^2 Adjusted
1987	94	0.1064 (4.467)*	0.6927 (10.543)*	54.45%
1988	91	-0.0775 (-1.147)*	1.3097 (5.235)*	22.49
1989	89	-0.0355 (1.742)***	0.8727 (9.626)*	50.74
1990	85	0.0019 (0.095)	0.7429 (9.055)*	48.79
1991	91	0.1353 (6.103)*	0.2828 (3.835)*	13.10
1992	89	0.0766 (3.291)*	0.7426 (7.835)*	40.43
1987 - 1992	544	0.0756 (6.410)*	0.6652 (16.19)*	32.43

[i]Heteroskedasticity—consistent t statistics—are within parenthesis.
*Significant at alpha = 0.01.
**Significant at alpha = 0.05.
***Significant at alpha = 0.10.
ROE = rate of return on equity.

Panel B
Model 2: $ROE_{it+1} = B_0 + B_1 ROE_{it} + B_2 FRTR_{it} + e''_{it}$

Year	Number of Firms	B_0[i]	B_1	B_2	R^2 Adjusted
1987	86	0.1026 (3.622)*	0.8282 (15.581)*	-0.0009 (-2.347)**	78.56%
1988	83	-0.2855 (-2.260)*	1.6121 (5.663)*	0.0027 (1.938)**	26.95
1989	81	-0.0076 (-0.194)	0.9431 (8.929)*	0.0005 (1.506)	50.67
1990	77	-0.0134 (-0.437)	0.7864 (8.470)*	0.00001 (0.043)	48.96
1991	74	0.1820 (4.974)*	0.2388 (2.999)*	-0.0005 (1.097)	9.78
1992	71	0.0388 (1.724)**	0.8946 (6.718)*	-0.00004 (-0.086)	38.36
87-92	537	0.0394 (1.724)**	0.6702 (16.381)*	0.0009 (1.501)	34.11

[i]Heteroskedasticity—consistent t statistics—are within parentheses.
*Significant at alpha = 0.01.
**Significant at alpha = 0.05.

Exhibit 2.3
Multinationality and Market Value

Panel A Model 3: $MV_{it} = Y_0 + Y_1 BV_{it} + e_{it}$

Year	Number of Firms	Y_0 (i)	Y_1	R^2 Adjusted
1987	120	27.6402 (7.565)*	0.5177 (4.277)*	12.59%
1988	120	30.9718 (9.024)*	0.5829 (5.389)*	18.94
1989	118	32.8444 (7.789)*	0.7544 (5.618)*	20.57
1990	112	34.3666 (8.913)*	0.3176 (7.556)*	24.77
1991	118	34.3477 (9.910)*	0.6404 (5.470)*	9.82
1992	117	33.3477 (9.910)*	0.6404 (5.470)*	19.82

(i)Heteroskedasticity—consistent *t* statistics—are within parentheses.
*Significant at alpha = 0.01. **Significant at alpha = 0.05.
MV_{it} = Market value of common equity per share for firm *i* at the end of year *t*.
BV_{it} = Book value of common equity per share for firm *i* at the end of year *t*.

Panel B Model 4: $MV_{it} = Y_0 + (Y_1 + Y_2 ROE_{it}) * BV_{it} + e'_{it}$

Year	Number of Firms	Y_0 (i)	Y_1	Y_2	R^2 Adjusted
1987	98	22.422 (5.537)*	0.4161 (3.422)*	1.8836 (5.398)*	32.71%
1988	100	26.021 (8.303)*	0.4105 (4.147)*	2.2661 (6.471)*	45.02
1989	96	32.7853 (6.675)*	0.6405 (3.940)*	1.0816 (2.589)*	25.16
1990	93	29.8169 (6.539)*	0.3268 (2.305)*	2.8719 (4.600)*	19.37
1991	97	33.9716 (6.343)*	0.5105 (3.256)*	0.9207 (1.721)**	8.20
1992	99	33.6381 (8.776)*	0.5888 (4.941)*	1.0625 (1.998)*	21.78
1987 1992	584	30.435 (8.776)*	0.5888 (4.941)*	1.0625 (1.998)*	21.78

(i)Heteroskedasticity—consistent *t* statistics—are within parentheses.
*Significant at alpha = 0.01. **Significant at alpha = 0.05.
***Significant at alpha = 0.10.
MV_{it} = Market value of common equity per share for firm *i* at the end of year *t*.
BV_{it} = Book value of common equity per share for firm *i* at the end of year *t*.

Exhibit 2.3 (Continued)

Panel C

Model 5: $MV_{it} = V_0 + (V_1 + V_2 ROE_{it} + V_3 FRTR) * BV_{it} + e''_{it}$

Year	No. of Firms	$V^{(i)}_0$	V_1	V_2	V_3	R^2 Adj.
1987	98	20.9448 (5.259)*	0.0935 (1.538)**	1.9794 (5.798)*	0.0108 (2.532)*	34.98%
1988	93	26.1471 (8.093)*	0.1932 (1.667)**	2.4421 (6.401)*	0.0060 (1.766)*	46.35
1989	90	23.0869 (5.467)*	0.4114 (2.117)*	4.9387 (7.132)*	0.0012 (2.303)*	49.25
1990	88	29.9840 (6.362)*	0.0928 (6.401)*	2.883 (4.571)*	0.0064 (1.742)**	20.52
1991	96	33.009 (5.846)*	0.2199 (2.896)*	1.0097 (1.748)*	0.0089 (1.717)**	8.98
1992	92	32.7814 (7.889)*	0.4263 (2.174)*	1.1586 (1.882)*	0.0043 (1.163)***	21.79
1987 1992	558	28.286 (9.097)*	0.1528 (1.837)**	1.9088 (9.709)*	0.0103 (5.431)*	27.71

(i)Heteroskedasticity—consistent t statistics—are within parentheses.
*Significant at alpha = 0.01.
**Significant at alpha = 0.05.
MV_{it} = Market value of common equity per share for firm i at the end of year t.
ROE_{it} = Rate of return on equity for firm i at the end of year t.
BV_{it} = Book value of common equity per share for firm i at the end of year t.
$FRTR_{it}$ = Foreign revenues/total revenues for firm i at the end of year t.

The results suggest that a better understanding of the role of accounting variables in the determination of firm value requires a consideration of multinationality as an unbooked or hidden asset. Basically, the pricing of securities by investors requires a proper consideration of a firm's multinationality.

NOTES

1. Jane A. Ou, "The Information Content of Nonearnings Accounting Numbers as Earnings Predictors," *Journal of Accounting Research* (Spring 1990): 144–163.

2. J. A. Ou and S. H. Penman, "Financial Statement Analysis and Prediction of Stock Returns," *Journal of Accounting and Economics* 11 (1989): 295–325.

3. H. Yang, J. Wansley, and W. Lane, "Stock Market Recognition of Multinationality of a Firm and International Events," *Journal of Business Finance and Accounting* 12 (1985): 263–274.

4. J. A. Ohlson, "Earnings, Book Values, and Dividends in Security Valuation," Working Paper, Columbia University, February 1991.

5. J. A. Ohlson, "Accounting Earnings, Book Value, and Dividends: The Theory of the Clean Surplus Equation," Working Paper, Columbia University, 1988.

6. S. H. Penman, "Return to Fundamentals," *Journal of Accounting, Auditing and Finance* (Fall 1992): 465–483.

7. V. L. Bernard, "Accounting-Based Valuation Models, Determinants of Market-to-Book Ratios, and Implications for Financial Analysis," Working Paper, University of Michigan, June 1993.

REFERENCES

Agmon, T., and D. Lessard. "Investor Recognition of Corporate International Diversification." *Journal of Finance* 12 (1979): 1049–1055.

Bernard, V. L. "Accounting-Based Valuation Models, Determinants of Market-to-Book Ratios, and Implications for Financial Statement Analysis." Working Paper, University of Michigan, June 1993.

Errunza, V., and L. Senbet. "International Corporate Diversification, Market Valuation and Size Adjusted Evidence." *Journal of Finance* (May 1981): 717–743.

Ohlson, J. A. "Earnings, Book Values, and Dividends in Security Valuation." Working Paper, Columbia University, February 1991.

Ohlson, J. A. "Accounting Earnings, Book Value, and Dividends: The Theory of the Clean Surplus Equation." Working Paper, Columbia University, 1988.

Ou, Jane A. "The Information Content of Nonearnings Accounting Numbers as Earnings Predictors." *Journal of Accounting Research* (Spring 1990): 144–163.

Ou, J. A., and S. H. Penman. "Financial Statement Analysis and the Evaluation of Market-to-Book Ratios." Working Paper, University of California at Berkeley, April 1993.

Ou, J. A., and S. H. Penman. "Accounting Measurement, Price-Earnings Ratio, and the Information Content of Security Prices." *Journal of Accounting Research* (Supplement 1989): 111–144.

Ou, J. A., and S. H. Penman. "Financial Statement Analysis and Prediction of Stock Returns." *Journal of Accounting and Economics* 11 (1989): 295–325.

Penman, S. H. "Return to Fundamentals." *Journal of Accounting, Auditing and Finance* (Fall 1992): 465–483.

Sullivan, Daniel. "Measuring the Degree of Internationalization of a Firm." *Journal of International Business Studies* 25 (1994): 325–342.

Tsetsekos, George P. "Multinationality and Common Stock Offering." *Journal of International Financial Management and Accounting* 3 (1991): 1–16.

White, H. "A Heteroskedasticity-Consistent Covariance Matrix Estimator and a Direct Test for Heteroskedasticity." *Econometrica* (May 1980): 1425–1460.

Yang, H., J. Wansley, and W. Lane. "Stock Market Recognition of Multinationality of a Firm and International Events." *Journal of Business Finance and Accounting* 12 (1985): 263–274.

3

Multinationality and Financial Performance

INTRODUCTION

The level of the degree of internationalization of most large U.S. firms has been increasing steadily, ranging from 10 to over 90 percent of total operations. One question frequently asked is if these foreign operations make any difference in the firm performance. Results from the financial performance effects of multinationality, however, have been inconsistent.[1] The studies reported either a positive, indeterminate, or negative relationship. Although the disarray may be easily attributed to the different measures used for both the degree of internationalization (DOI) and financial performance, it may be due to a misspecification of the nature of the linear relationship. Whereas most studies examined a simple linear relationship between DOI and financial performance, this chapter argues for the existence of a nonmonotonic relationship. Basically, it is hypothesized that the rate of return on assets declines, then increases, and finally decreases slightly as the degree of internationalization, measured by foreign revenues/total revenues, increases.

THEORETICAL FRAMEWORK

The multinational firm is a collection of valuable options and generates arbitrage profits that enhances its value.[2] The arbitrage benefits result

Exhibit 3.1
The Reported Direction of the Relationship between Degree of Internationalization and the Financial Performance of the Firm

Positive	Indeterminate	Negative
Vernon [1971]	Horst [1973]	Siddharthan & Lall [1982]
Dunning [1985]	Hughes, Logue & Sweeny [1975]	Kumar [1984]
Grant [1987]	Buckley, Dunning & Pearce [1977]	Michel & Shaked [1986]
Grant, Jammine & Thomas [1988]	Rugman, Lecraw & Booth [1985]	Shaked [1986]
Daniels & Bracker [1989]	Yoshihara [1985]	Collins [1990]
Geringer, Beamish & daCosta [1989]	Buhner [1987]	

Source: Daniel Sullivan, ''Measuring the Degree of Internationalization of a Firm,'' *Journal of International Business Studies* 25, no. 2 (1994): 327. Reprinted with permission.

from (a) the exploitation of various institutional imperfections, (b) timing options, (c) technology options, and (d) staging options.[3,4] Better financing bargains, as well as capital availibility are also possible through internationalization. In addition, this ability of the multinational firm to exploit interrelationships between different segments, geographical areas, or related industries, coupled with the benefits of economies of scale, scope, and experience, suggest a positive association between dependence on foreign operations and profit performance.[5,6] The rush to test this simple relationship, however, has been inconclusive, with some studies showing a positive relationship, a negative relationship, or an indeterminate relationship. These studies are identified and summarized in Exhibits 3.1 and 3.2.

What these inconsistent results suggest is that the relationship is far from a simple linear one. It is due to the failure of theories of foreign investment to specify whether some optimal degree of multinationality of a firm's operations exists.[7] The thesis of ''more multinationality is better'' should hold only after a certain level of multinationality, and until the firm reaches an optimum combination of domestic to foreign operations. What the simple relationship implicitly says is that a firm gains immediately with the lowest level of multinationality and continues

Exhibit 3.2
Summary of Empirical Studies of the Relationship between Financial Performance and the Degree of Internationalization

Study	Sample	Measure of DOI	Measure of Performance	Report
Vernon [1971]	The Fortune 500 in 1964	*FSTS*	ROS ROA	MNCs earned higher ROS and higher post-tax ROA than did non-MNCs.
Horst [1973]	1191 United States Industrial firms	*FSTS*	Net profits	After controlling for firm size, unable to discriminate MNCs from non-MNCs on basis of net profits.
Hughes, Logue & Sweeny [1975]	46 U.S. MNCs 50 U.S. non-MNCs	*FSTS*	*Beta*; Risk-adjusted returns	MNCs had higher risk-adjusted returns to shareholders, but lower average returns to shareholders as well as a lower average *beta*.
Siddharthan & Lall [1982]	The 500 and 100 largest U.S. and non-U.S. MNCs, respectively, in 1972	*FSTS*	Firm growth	Controlling for firm size, advertising intensity, R&D intensity, scale economies, and profitability indicates that DOI had a negative effect on the rate of firm growth.
Kumar [1984]	672 British firms, 1972-1976	*FSTS*	ROS, ROA	MNCs outperformed non-MNCs for both ROS and ROA; however, OLS revealed negative but nonsignificant relationship between *FSTS* and profits.
Buckley, Dunning & Pearce [1977]	The 636 and 866 largest MNCs of the world, respectively, for 1972 and 1977	*FSTS*	ROA	Results are"somewhat inconsistent"; while statistically significant in 1972 for full sample, relationship was insignificant for the full and U.S. sample in 1977.
Dunning [1985]	188 large British MNCs, 1979	*FSTS*	ROS	Degree of multinationality had a positive but statistically insignificant relationship with ROS.
Yoshihara [1985]	The largest 118 Japanese firms	*FSTS*	ROE	MNCs outperformed non-MNCS in terms of ROS but the differences were not statistically significant.
Rugman, Lecraw & Booth [1985]	The 50, 50, 20, 10, and 24, respectively, largest U.S., European, Japanese, Canadian, and Third World MNCs	*FSTS*	ROE	No evidence of excessive profits for MNCs. Most MNCs had ROE between 10%-14%, which were similar to the ROE of domestic firms of similar size.

Exhibit 3.2 (Continued)

Study	Sample	Measure of DOI	Measure of Performance	Report
Shaked [1986]	58 U.S. MNCs, 43 non-U.S. MNCs for 1980-1982	*FSTS*	ROA, *Beta*	ROA did not differ significantly between MNCs and domestic firms. MNCs had lower systematic risk, odds of insolvency, and equity variability, but also experienced lower sales growth than domestic firms.
Michel & Shaked [1986]	58 U.S. MNCs and 43 non-U.S. MNCs for 1973-1982	*FSTS*	Risk-adjusted returns	Risk-adjusted returns to stockholders were higher for domestic firms than for MNCs.
Grant [1987]	304 British firms for 1968-1984	*FSTS*	Sales growth; ROS, ROA, ROE	Internationalization was positively associated with superior profitability over a period of thirteen years.
Buhner [1987]	40 West German firms	*FSTS*	Risk-adjusted returns, ROE, ROA	Single business firms with high degrees of internationalization outperformed other firms. Performance between others was not significantly different.
Grant, Jammine & Thomas [1988]	304 British firms for 1972-1984	*FSTS*	ROA	No evidence of an association between high levels of DOI and a significant downturn in profitability.
Daniels & Bracker [1989]	116 U.S. MNCs	*FSTS*; *FATA*	ROS, ROA	Performance improved significantly as *FSTS* and *FATA* increased to 50%. While not a significant association, performance seemed to fall as *FSTS* and *FATA* increased beyond this threshold.
Geringer, Beamish & daCosta [1989]	The largest 100 U.S. and 100 European MNCs of 1981	*FSTS*	ROS, ROA	Financial performance improved monotonically as *FSTS* grew but peaked and declined when *FSTS* crossed the revealed threshold of 60%-80% of internationalization.
Collins [1990]	150 firms of the Fortune 500	*FSTS*	Total risk, Leverage, *Beta*	Performance of MNCs with developed country DFI was equal to domestic firms but the performance of MNCs with operations in developing countries was inferior to other MNCs and domestic firms.

Notes: ROS = Rate of return in equity. OLS = Ordinary least squares.
ROA = Rate of return on assets. DFI = Direct foreign investment.

Source: Daniel Sullivan, "Measuring the Degree of Internationalization of a Firm," *Journal of International Business Studies* 25, no. 2 (1994): 328–329. Reprinted with permission.

to improve its financial performance until it has no domestic operations at all. One more logical thesis would be that the entry of a firm in the multinational arena is costly up to a first level of combination of domestic to foreign operations, then is profitable up to a second level beyond which performance will stagnate or decline. It implies that firm performance will be negatively related to lower and higher ranges of multinationality and positively related to middle ranges of multinationality. In other words, a nonmonotonic relationship is implied:

> H_1: There will be a negative relationship between a firm's performance and degree of internationalization held at a lower or higher range, and a positive relationship for a middle range.

This hypothesis holds if multinationality is measured by foreign revenues/total revenues. Opposite signs are expected if multinationality is measured by foreign assets/total assets.

DEGREE OF INTERNATIONALIZATION AND FIRM PERFORMANCE

The hypothesis states that firm performance, as measured by the rate of return on assets, is associated with the degree of internationalization, as measured by foreign revenues/total revenues, in a piecewise linear fashion. Control for size is accomplished by introducing the logarithm of assets as a control variable.

The piecewise linear regression model allowing for two changes in the slope coefficient of the degree of internationalization is as follows:

$$\begin{aligned}\text{PERF}_i = a_1 + a_2\text{DOI1}_i + a_3\text{DOI2}_i + a_4\text{DOI3}_i \\ + \text{LA}_i + u_i, \end{aligned} \qquad (1)$$

where

PERF_i = Financial performance of a firm as measured by the rate of return on assets,

DOI_i = Degree of internalization, measured by foreign revenues/total revenues, defined as follows:

if $DOI_i <$ level one, then $DOI1_i = DOI_i$;
if $DOI_i >$ level one, then $DOI1_i =$ level one;
if $DOI_i <$ level one, then $DOI2_i = 0$;
if (level one $\leqslant DOI_i <$ level two), then $DOI2_i = DOI_i -$ level one;
if $DOI_i \geqslant$ level two, then $DOI2_i =$ level two $-$ level one;
if $DOI_i <$ level two, then $DOI3_i = 0$;
if DOI $\geqslant$ level two, then $DOI3_i = DOI_i -$ level two.

The first stage of the analysis is to determine the turning points of level one and two of DOI. The multivariate adaptive regression spline (MARS) methodology is used for the determination of these two levels of DOI.[8,9]

SAMPLE SELECTION AND DESCRIPTIVE STATISTICS

Since 1979, *Forbes* has annually ranked the ''most international'' 100 American manufacturing and service firms on the basis of foreign revenues. All the firms in *Forbes'* classification from 1987 to 1993 were included in our sample, resulting in 612 firm-year observations. All the other variables were obtained from the Compustat Annual Primary-Secondary-Tertiary database.

FIRST EMPIRICAL RESULTS

The first empirical results are based on DOI as foreign revenues/total revenues. The MARS technique fits a model in the form of an expansion in product line spline function of predictors. The two thresholds identified by the program were 34 and 47 percent for foreign revenues/total revenues. They were used as level one and level two in the piecewise linear regression between, on one hand, the rate of return on assets of multinational firms, and on the other hand, the three ranges of degree of internationalization and the logarithm of total assets. Basically, DOI1 covers the foreign revenues/total revenues between 0 and 34 percent,

Exhibit 3.3
Piecewise Linear Ordinary Least-Squares Regression of Rate of Return on Assets on Degree of Internationalization[1]

Intercept	0.3072
	(12.796)
$DOI1_2$	-0.00082
	(-2.185)*
DOI2	0.0011
	(4.183)*
DOI3	-0.0009
	(-2.682)*
LA_3	-0.0242
	(-13.978)*
F	63.130
R^2	28.88%

[1]Numbers in parentheses are *t* statistics computed according to White (1980).
[2]DOI = Degree of internationalization, measured as foreign revenues/total revenues.
[3]ROI = Rate of return on assets.
*Significant at the 99% confidence level.

DOI2 covers the range between 34 and 47 percent, and DOI3 covers the area above 47 percent.

Exhibit 3.3 reports the piecewise linear regression results. As suggested by the main hypothesis in this study, the relationship between firm performance, as measured by the rate of return on assets, and the degree of internationalization, as measured by foreign revenues/total revenues is a nonmonotonic one. It is negative at a low range of DOI (0–34%), positive at a higher range (34–47%), and negative at levels superior to 47 percent. Basically, for each 1 percent increase in multinationality between 0 and 34 percent, firm performance, in terms of rate of return on assets, declines respectively by an average of 0.0082. For each 1 percent increase in multinationality between 34 and 47 percent, firm performance increases by 0.0011. As multinationality increases beyond 47 percent, firm performance decreases slightly by 0.0009. The results are consistent with the optimal degrees of multinationality hypothesis. The results are different from most studies, which showed a monotonic relationship, and the two studies that showed only one threshhold of 50 percent[10] and 60 percent.[11]

SECOND EMPIRICAL RESULTS

The second empirical results are based on DOI as foreign assets/total assets. The MARS technique identified one threshold of 45 percent for foreign assets/total assets. It was used as level one in the piecewise linear regression between, on one hand, the rate of return on assets of multinational firms, and on the other hand, the two ranges of the degree of internationalization and the logarithm of assets. Basically DOI1 covers the foreign assets/total assets between 0 and 45 percent, and DOI2 covers the area above 45 percent. Exhibit 3.4 reports the piecewise linear regression results. As suggested by the hypothesis, the relationship between firm performance, as measured by the rate of return on assets, and the degree of internationalization, as measured by foreign assets/total assets, is a nonmonotonic one. It is positive at middle ranges going from 0 to 45 percent, and negative at levels superior to 45 percent. Basically, for every 1 percent increase in multinationality between 0 and 45 percent, firm performance, in terms of rate of return on assets, increases by an average of 2.757. For each increase beyond 45 percent firm performance decreases by −3.905. The results are again consistent with the optimal degree of multinationality hypothesis. The amount of foreign assets/total assets that can generate an adequate performance for a multinational firm cannot exceed an optimal amount. This chapter shows that the optimal amount is 45 percent.

CONCLUSIONS

The results of this study show a nonmonotonic relationship between firm performance, as measured by the rate of return on assets, and DOI,

Exhibit 3.4
Piecewise Linear Ordinary Least-Squares Regression of Rate of Return on Assets on Foreign Assets/Total Assets[1]

Intercept	0.290605
	(15.481)*
$DOI1_2$	0.000522
	(2.757)*
DOI2	-0.001545
	(-3.905)*
LA_3	-0.02453
	(-14.253)*
F	83.80
R2	29.39%

[1]Numbers in parentheses are *t* statistics.
[2]DOI – Degree of internationalization, measured as foreign assets/total assets.
[3]LA = Logarithm of total assets.

as measured by foreign revenues/total revenues. They support the existence of a dual threshhold point that better defines the nature of the relationship, with a negative relationship under 34 percent, a positive relationship between 34 and 47 percent, and a negative relationship for a degree of internationalization higher than 47 percent. The ''more multinationality is better'' thesis is verified only in the range defined by the threshhold of 34 and 47 percent of foreign revenues/total revenues. Basically, there is a minimum and a maximum combination of foreign to domestic operations that defines the relationship between firm performance and degree of internationalization. They also support the existence of one threshold point that defines the nature of the relationship with a positive relationship under 45 percent and a negative relationship above 45 percent of foreign assets/total assets.

Further verification of the results are necessary for the construction of a more complete theory of the relationship between firm performance and multinationality. The replications may be done on a different sample than the "100 most multinational" firms, a different time period, and different measures of firm performance and DOI.

NOTES

1. Daniel Sullivan, "Measuring the Degree of Internationalization of a Firm," *Journal of International Business Studies* 25, no. 2 (1994): 325–342.
2. George P. Tsetsekos, "Multinationality and Common Stock Offering," *Journal of International Financial Management and Accounting* 3 (1991): 1–16.
3. C. Baldwin, "The Capital Factor: Competition for Capital in Global Environment," in M. Porter (ed.), *Competition in Global Industries* (Boston: Harvard Business School Press, 1986), 184–223.
4. Bruce Kogut, "Foreign Direct Investment as a Sequential Process," in C. Kindelberger and D. Andretsh (eds.), *The Multinational Corporation in the 1980s* (Cambridge, Mass.: The MIT Press, 1983), 38–56.
5. Michael E. Porter, *Competitive Advantage* (New York: Free Press, 1985).
6. Bruce Kogut, "Designing Global Strategies: Profiting from Operational Flexibility," *Sloan Management Review* 27 (1985): 27–38.
7. J. Michael Geringer, Paul W. Beamish, and Richard C. daCosta, "Diversification Strategy and Internationalization: Implications for MNE Performance," *Strategic Management Journal* 10 (1989): 109–119.
8. J. H. Friedman, "Multivariate Adaptive Regression Splines," *The Annals of Statistics* 19 (1991): 1–50.
9. P.A.W. Lewis, and J. G. Stevens, "Nonlinear Modeling of Time Series Using Multivariate Adaptive Regression Splines (MARS)," *Journal of the American Statistical Association* (December 1991): 864–877.
10. John D. Daniel and John Bracker, "Profit Performance: Do Foreign Operations Make a Difference?" *Management International Review* 29 (1989): 46–56.
11. Geringer, Beamish, and daCosta, "Diversification Strategy and Internationalization: Implications for MNE Performance," op. cit.

REFERENCES

Baldwin, C. ''The Capital Factor: Competition for Capital in Global Environment.'' In M. Porter (ed.), *Competition in Global Industries* (Boston: Harvard Business School Press, 1986), 184–223.

Buckley, Peter J., John H. Dunning, and Robert B. Pearce. ''The Influence of Firm Size, Industry, Nationality, and Degree of Multinationality in the Growth and Profitablity of the World's Largest Firms.'' *Weltwirtschaftliches Archiv* 114 (1977): 243–257.

Buhner, Rolf. ''Assessing International Diversification of West German Corporations.'' *Strategic Management Journal* 8 (1987): 25–37.

Business Week, ''International Scoreboard of U.S. Corporations.'' (March 22, 1985): 158–162.

Collins, J. Markham. ''A Market Performance Comparison of U.S. Firms Active in Domestic, Developed and Developing Countries.'' *Journal of International Business Studies* 21 (1990): 289–300.

Daniel, John D., and John Bracker. ''Profit Performance: Do Foreign Operations Make a Difference?'' *Management International Review* 29 (1989): 46–56.

Dunning, John H. ''The Determinants of International Production.'' *Oxford Economic Papers* 25 (November 1985): 289–336.

Eiteman, D., and A. Stonehill. *Multinational Business Finance* (Boston: Addison-Wesley, 1986).

Friedman, J. H. ''Multivariate Adaptive Regression Splines.'' *The Annals of Statistics* 19 (1991): 1–50.

Geringer, J. Michael, Paul W. Beamish, and Richard C. daCosta. ''Diversification Strategy and Internationalization: Implications for MNE Performance.'' *Strategic Management Journal* 10 (1989): 109–119.

Giavazzi, F., and A. Stonehill. *Limiting Exchange Rate Flexibility: The European Monetary System* (Cambridge, Mass.: MIT Press, 1989).

Grant, Robert M. ''Multinationality and Performance Among British Manufacturing Companies.'' *Journal of International Business Studies* 18 (1987): 79–89.

Grant, Robert M., P. Jammine Azar, and Howard Thomas. ''Diversity, Diversification, and Profitability among British Manufacturing Companies, 1972–1984.'' *Academy of Management Journal* 31 (1988): 771–801.

Horst, Thomas E. "Firm and Industry Determinants of the Decision to Invest Abroad." *Review of Economics and Statistics* 54 (August 1973): 258–266.

Hughes, J. S., D. E. Logue, and R. J. Sweeney. "Corporate International Diversification and Market Assigned Measures of Risk and Diversification." *Journal of Financial and Quantitative Analysis* 10 (November 1965): 627–637.

Kogut, Bruce. "Designing Global Strategies: Profiting from Operational Flexibility." *Sloan Management Review* 27 (1985): 27–38.

Kogut, Bruce. "Foreign Direct Investment as a Sequential Process." In C. Kindelberger and D. Andretsh (eds.), *The Multinational Corporation in the 1980s* (Cambridge, Mass.: The MIT Press, 1983), 38–56.

Kumar, Manmohan S. *Growth Acquisition and Investment: An Analysis of the Growth of Industrial Firms and Their Overseas Activities* (Cambridge, U.K.: Cambridge University Press, 1984).

Lewis, P.A.W., and J. G. Stevens. "Nonlinear Modeling of Time Series Using Multivariate Adaptive Regression Splines (MARS)." *Journal of the American Statistical Association* (December 1991): 864–877.

Michel, Allen, and Israel Shaked. "Domestic Corporations: Financial Performance and Characteristics." *Journal of International Business Studies* 18 (1986): 89–100.

Porter, Michael E. *Competitive Advantage* (New York: Free Press, 1985).

Rugman, Alan M., Donald J. Lecraw, and Lawrence D. Booth. *International Business: Firm and Environment* (New York: McGraw-Hill, 1985).

Shaked, Israel. "Are Multinational Corporations Safer?" *Journal of International Business Studies* 17 (1986): 75–80.

Shapiro, A. *Multinational Financial Management,* 3rd edition. (Boston: Allyn and Bacon, 1989).

Siddharthan, Natteri, and Sanjaya Lall. "Recent Growth of the Largest U.S. Multinationals." *Oxford Bulletin of Economics and Statistics* 44 (1982): 1–13.

Sullivan, Daniel. "Measuring the Degree of Internationalization of a Firm." *Journal of International Business Studies* 25, no. 2 (1994): 325–342.

Tsetsekos, George P. "Multinationality and Common Stock Offering." *Journal of International Financial Management and Accounting* 3 (1991): 1–16.

Vernon, Raymond. *Sovereignty at Bay: The Multinational Spread of U.S. Enterprises* (New York: Basic Books, 1971).

White, H. "A Heteroskedasticity-Consistent Covariance Matrix Estimator and a Direct Test for Heteroskedasticity." *Econometrica* 10 (1980): 1425–1460.

Yoshihara, Hiro. "Multinational Growth of Japanese Manufacturing Enterprises in the Postwar Period." *Proceedings of the Fuji International Conference on Business History* (Tokyo: University of Tokyo Press, 1985).

4

Multinationality and Prediction Performance of Earnings Forecasts

INTRODUCTION

Rivera[1] shows that the accuracy of (consensus in) analysts' earnings forecasts of U.S. domestic companies is less than for U.S. multinational corporations. This study extends Rivera's analysis by investigating whether the accuracy of (consensus in) analysts' earnings forecasts differs between thirty-one U.S. multinationals with substantial operations in developed countries and twenty-six U.S. multinationals with substantial operations in developing countries. Twenty-one U.S. firms with no international operations are also examined. The results indicate that the accuracy of analysts' earnings forecasts differs across the three groups of firms: U.S. firms with no international operations are the most accurate, whereas U.S. firms with significant operations in developing countries are the least accurate (difference significant at alpha = 0.10 level). No significant differences in consensus were noted across the three groups.

This chapter was adapted with permission of JAI Press from Ahmed Riahi-Belkaoui, "Prediction Performance of Earnings Forecasts of U.S. Firms Active in Developed and Developing Countries," *Advances in Accounting in Emerging Economics* 3 (1995): 85–97.

BACKGROUND AND HYPOTHESES

Prior research suggests that analysts' forecasts of earnings are associated with significant security price revisions. The more accurate the earnings prediction, the more information content the management forecast carries.[2] Various factors are expected to influence the accuracy of analysts's earnings forecast, including industry, size of firm, variability of earnings, and forecasting horizon. Also, Rivera[3] finds that the accuracy of analysts' earnings forecasts and their level of consensus are significantly lower for U.S. domestic than for U.S. multinational firms.

Rivera[4] does not distinguish between U.S. firms with significant international operations in developed countries and those with significant international operations in developing countries. This difference is important given the Markham Collins[5] evidence that U.S. domestic firms and U.S. multinationals operating in developed countries exhibit higher returns and risk than U.S. multinationals operating in developing countries. Based on these findings, errors in forecasting for developed country firms and the dispersion of these forecasts around a consensus mean would be comparatively smaller than those for a domestic firm and a developing country firm. In addition, an international firm with operations in a developing country operates in a more ''demanding'' environment than a domestic firm, possibly leading to higher forecast errors and dispersion of these forecasts around the mean for these firms.

Two hypotheses are tested:

H_1: The accuracy of analysts' earnings forecasts is not significantly different between U.S. domestic firms, U.S. multinationals with operations in developed countries, and U.S. multinationals with international operations in developing countries.

H_2: The consensus in analysts' estimates is not similar across the three groups.

RESEARCH DESIGN

Sample

Sample selection followed the same procedures as Markham Collins.[6] First, an initial set of 230 firms, numbers 1 to 230 of the 1991 *Fortune*

500, was selected. Although the selection appears arbitrary, it is motivated by the need to secure firms of approximately equal size and a fairly even distribution between the three categories of international involvment.

Second, given the 10 percent threshhold set by *Statement of Financial Accounting Standards Number 14* (SFAS No. 14), firms not reporting both 10 percent of revenues and assets as foreign in 1988–90 were classified as domestic (group 1). Those meeting the 10 percent test were classified as multinationals.

Third, the U.S. Department of Commerce classifies countries as developed or developing. Developing countries include Latin American countries, African countries (excluding South Africa), Middle Eastern countries, and Asian and Pacific countries (excluding Japan). This distinction was used to classify subsidiaries of the multinational firms (obtained in step 2) as developed or developing.[7] Multinational firms with at least 25 percent of their total foreign subsidiaries and at least eight subsidiaries in developing countries were classified as having a substantial presence in developing countries (group 3). All remaining multinationals were classified as developed country firms (group 2).[8]

Fourth, the original sample was restricted to firms with available data on CRSP, IBES, and Compustat. Absolute forecast errors in excess of 100 percent were deleted from the sample.

The final sample includes twenty one group 1 firms, thirty-one group 2 firms, and twenty-six group 3 firms (Appendix 4.A lists the firm names).

Dependendent Variables

The financial analysts' predictions of annual earnings per share (EPS) for the seventy-eight firms in the sample and the actual earnings per share reported by the firms were used to determine the three dependent variables: percentage of error, absolute percentage of error, and coefficient of variation. They are computed as follows. First, percentage of error is

$$PE_{ijt} = (FE_{ijt} - AE_{ij})/AE_{ij}. \qquad (1)$$

Second, absolute percentage of error is

$$APE_{ijt} = (FE_{ijt} - AE_{ij})/AE_{ij}, \tag{2}$$

where

PE_{ijt} = Percentage of forecast error for firm i for year j for forecast horizon t;
APE_{ijt} = Absolute percentage forecast error for firm i for year j for forecast horizon t;
FE_{ijt} = is the mean analyst earnings forecast for firm i for year j at time t;
AE_{if} = Actual annual EPS for company i for year j;
j = Each of the 1988–1990 years covered in the study;
t = Forecasting horizon, three, six, or nine months preceding the month that actual EPS is reported.

Coefficient of Variation

The coefficient of variation is used as a measure of consensus in analysts' EPS forecasts:

$$CV_{ijt} = o_{FE}/FE_{ijt},$$

where

CV_{ijt} = Coefficient of variation of forecasts to measure the agreement or disagreement among analysts when predicting earnings of company i for year j at time t, the smaller this coefficient, the higher the agreement among the analysts about a company's estimated future earnings;
o_{FE} = is the standard deviation of the analysts' earnings forecasts.

Forecast data are derived from Institutional Brokers Estimate System (IBES), a service of Lynch, Jones, and Ryan.

Covariates

Four covariates were used: size, systematic risk, price-earnings ratio, and institutional membership.

Size is used as covariate because previous work has shown it affects performance[9] and variability in performance.[10] The natural logarithm of year-end assets is used as a proxy for firm size. Logarithm transformation is justified when values of one variable are highly skewed—as is often the case with size—because the extreme values can strongly affect correlations with other variables.[11,12]

One influence on prediction performance may be the differences in systematic risk across firms in the three groups. Multinational investment can be used for risk diversification. In addition, Barefield and Comiskey[13] show that forecast errors are associated with systematic risk. For each firm in the sample, market model coefficients were estimated, using monthly CRSP returns over the 1988–1990 period examined.

Price-earnings ratio was used as a covariate based on Copeland and Weston's[14] evidence that higher price-earnings ratios reflect more favorable earnings growth prospects.

Finally, institutional ownership was used as a covariate based on the finding that institutional ownership is positively correlated with the number of analysts following the firm. Institutional ownership was measured by the percentage of outstanding shares of stock held by banks, colleges, pension funds, insurance companies, and investment companies as calculated by Vickers Stock Research Corporation.

DATA ANALYSIS AND RESULTS

Analysis of covariance was used to test the relations between the earnings prediction performance of financial analysts and groups 1, 2, and 3. The model's covariates include systematic risk, price-earnings ratio, size, and institutional ownership.

Exhibit 4.1 reports the means, standard deviations, and correlations by firm group for the primary variables used in the study. Exhibits 4.2, 4.3, and 4.4 present results, respectively, for the percentage error, the absolute percentage error, and the coefficient of variation.

The results in Exhibits 4.2 and 4.3 suggest that the relation between firm groups and percentage of error or absolute percentage of error is

Exhibit 4.1
Means, Standard Deviations, and Correlation Coefficients of Variables by Firm Group

	Means (a)	Correlation						
		1	2	3	4	5	6	7
a. <u>Developing Country Group</u>								
1. Percentage of Error	0.0943 (0.233)	.	1.000	0.2750	0.1608	-0.1469	0.1187	0.2975
2. Absolute Percentage of Error	0.3281 (0.3843)	.	.	0.2750	0.1608	-0.1469	0.1187	0.2975
3. Coefficient of Variation	0.0455 (0.0424)	.	.	.	0.1043	0.1843	-0.2661	0.2538
4. Systematic Rick	1.1077 (0.1090)	.	.	.	.	0.2812	0.5753	0.2276
5. Assets (in millions)	4407 (2997)	.	.	.	.	.	0.3439	- 0.0003
6. Price/Earnings Ratio	20.8571 (10.3551)	.	.	.	.	.	.	0.2083
7. Institutional Ownership	58.7600 (16.5360)	.	.	.	.	.	.	.

	Means (a)	Correlation						
		1	2	3	4	5	6	7
a. <u>Developed Country Group</u>								
1. Percentage of Error	0.1154 (0.5941)	.	0.6880	0.1439	0.0032	0.1245	0.2857	-0.3603
2. Absolute Percentage of Error	0.3286 (0.6202)	.	.	-0.1019	-0.0797	0.2966	0.2857	-0.0637
3. Coefficient of Variation	0.6539 (0.1296)	.	.	.	0.4259	-0.2074	0.0751	-0.2494
4. Systematic Risk	1.0837 (0.1595)	.	.	.	.	-0.0718	0.1846	-0.0333
5. Assets (in millions)	16816 (37808)	.	.	.	.	.	-0.3766	-0.2749
6. Price/Earnings Ratio	20.2258 (12.2711)	.	.	.	.	.	.	0.1787
7. Institutional Ownership	57.2619 (14.3681)	.	.	.	.	.	.	.

Exhibit 4.1 (Continued)

	Means (a)	Correlation						
		1	2	3	4	5	6	7
a. <u>Domestic Firm Group</u>								
1. Percentage of Error	0.0369 (0.7029)	.	.000	0.1749	-0.1227	-0.0195	0.3833	0.1142
2. Absolute Percentage of Error	0.0153 (0.2782)	.	.	0.1749	-0.1227	-0.0195	0.3833	0.1142
3. Coefficient of Variation	0.0195 (0.0781)	.	.	.	0.0267	-0.1870	-0.0289	0.1256
4. Systematic Risk	1.1141 (0.1420)	.	.	.	.	0.2140	-0.0549	0.0495
5. Assets (in millions)	[illegible]9170 (34368)	.	.	.	.	.	-0.2644	- 0.3343
6. Price/Earnings Ratio	22.3864 (10.0442)	.	.	.	.	.	.	0.2864
7. Institutional Ownership	59.8485 (11.5410)	.		.	.	.	.	.

(a) Standard deviations are in parenthesis.

Exhibit 4.2
Results of the Overall Analysis of Covariance for Percentage of Error

Sources	DF	Mean Square	F Value	Pr > F
Model	6	1.334	1.88	0.0965*
Firm Group	2	1.720	2.42	0.0960*
Covariates				
1. Systematic risk	1	0.7617	1.07	0.3038
2. Price-Earnings Ratio	1	1.6685	2.35	0.1258
3. Size (log of Assets)	1	2.0340	2.87	0.0950
4. Institutional Ownership		0.0994	0.14	0.7093
Error	70	0.7099		
Corrected total	76			

*Significant at alpha = 0.10.

Exhibit 4.3
Results of the Overall Analysis of Covariance for Absolute Percentage of Error

Sources	DF	Mean Square	F Value	Pr > F
Model	5	1.0002	2.17	0.056*
Firm Group	2	1.2141	2.63	0.0791*
Covariates				
1. Systematic risk	1	0.7077	1.53	0.2197
2. Price-Earnings Ratio	1	1.683	3.65	0.0685*
3. Size (log of Assets)	1	1.163	2.52	0.1168
4. Institutional Ownership	1	0.0186	0.04	0.8412
Error	70	0.4691		
Corrected total	76			

*Significant at alpha = 0.10.

Exhibit 4.4
Results of the Overall Analysis of Covariance for Coefficient of Variation

Sources	DF	Mean Square	F Value	Pr > F
Model	6	0.0009	1.35	0.2491
Firm Group	2	0.0014	2.01	0.1410
Covariates				
1. Systematic risk	1	0.00002	0.03	0.8580
2. Price-earnings ratio	1	0.00013	0.19	0.6659
3. Size (log of sales)	1	0.0026	3.67	0.0594*
4. Institutional Ownership	1	0.00001	0.16	0.6939
Error	70	0.00071		
Corrected total	76			

*Significant at alpha = 0.05.

significant, suggesting that the accuracy of analysts' earnings forecasts differs significantly across the three groups.

The results in Exhibit 4.4 suggest, however, that the relation between firm groups and the coefficient of variation is not significant, suggesting similar levels of agreement in analysts' earnings forecasts for the three groups.

Exhibit 4.5 reports a mean comparison of the dependent variables for the three groups of firms. Consistent with the multivariate results, the univariate comparisons reveal no significant differences in the dispersion of analysts' EPS forecasts.

The comparison of absolute percentage forecast errors and percentage of error show that group 3 firms (those with significant operations in developing countries) are less accurate than those of group 2 (firms with significant international operations in developed countries) or group 1 (U.S. domestic firms).

DISCUSSION

Unlike previous results, ours show no differences for the earnings forecast errors for domestic and U.S. multinational firms with operations in developed countries. Rivera's study[15] did not make the distinction between investment in developed versus developing countries. Our study shows that the earnings forecast errors of financial analysts' earnings per share estimates are larger for U.S. multinational firms with significant international operations in developing countries than for domestic firms or U.S. multinational firms with significant international operations in developed countries. The results point to the unique characteristics associated with investments in developing countries versus developed countries as evidenced by (a) higher returns, performance measures, and risk measures for domestic and developed country firms relative to the developing country firms and (b) the less than perfect correlation between equity markets across national borders, with lower correlations with developing countries and higher correlations with developed countries. These characteristics translate into the higher forecasting errors of financial analysts' earnings per share estimates of firms with significant operations in developing countries.

Exhibit 4.5

Mean Comparisons of Dependent Variables for the Three Groups of Firms

	Lower Confidence Unit	Difference Between Means	Upper Confidence Unit	Significance (a)
1. Percentage of Error				
Group 3-Group 2	-0.1034	0.3468	0.7971	xxx
Group 3-Group 1	0.0327	0.5258	1.018	xxx
Group 2-Group 1	-0.2992	0.1789	0.6570	NS
2. Absolute Percentage of Error				
Group 3-Group 2	-0.0931	0.2699	0.6330	xxx
Group 3-Group 1	0.0513	0.4488	0.8464	xxx
Group 2-Group 1	-0.2066	0.1789	0.5644	NS
3. Coefficient of Variation				
Group 3-Group 2	-0.0121	0.0020	0.0163	NS
Group 3-Group 1	-0.0280	-0.0124	0.0031	NS
Group 2-Group 1	-0.0296	-0.0145	0.0006	NS

(a) xxx significant at alpha = 0.05; NS = not significant.

CONCLUSIONS

This study investigates the accuracy and dispersion among analysts' earnings forecasts for three groups of U.S. firms: those with no significant international operations, those with significant international operations in developed countries, and those with significant international operations in developing countries. The results indicate that domestic firms and firms with significant international operations in developed countries have more accurate earnings forecasts than firms with significant international operations in developing countries. Various conclusions can be reached.

First, the financial analysts' forecasts need to take into account the unique factors inherent to the developing countries' environment.

Second, the similarity of the forecast errors for domestic firms and firms with international operations in developed countries points to the increasing commonality of the economic environment in the United States and the developing countries.

Third, these results suggests the need to differentiate between multinational firms operating in developed countries and those operating in developing countries.

Future research should consider the removal of two major limitations of this study. First, a classification other than the U.S. Department of Commerce's classification of developed and developing countries should be used. Some measure of per capita GNP may make more sense than a classification based on geography. Second, a classification between developed and developing country investments based on an overall percentage of revenues or assets in developing countries may be tried to test the results of this study.

NOTES

1. Juan M. Rivera, ''Prediction Performance of Earnings Forecasts: The Case of U.S. Multinationals,'' *Journal of International Business Studies* 22 (1991): 265–288.

2. James M. Patell, ''Corporate Forecasts of Earnings per Share and Stock Price Behavior: Empirical Tests,'' *Journal of Accounting Research* (Autumn 1976): 246–276.

3. Rivera, "Prediction Performance of Earnings Forecasts: The Case of U.S. Multinationals," op. cit.

4. Ibid.

5. J. Markham Collins, "A Market Performance Comparison of U.S. Firms Active in Domestic, Developed, and Developing Countries," *Journal of International Business Studies* 21 (1990): 289–300.

6. Ibid.

7. The U.S. Department of Commerce's classification is used for reasons of comparability. It has also been used by Markham Collins (1990).

8. Better classification between developed and developing country investments based on assets or sales in the respective countries was not used because of the inability to secure a complete database.

9. M. Hall and L. Weiss, "Firm Size and Profitability," *Review of Economics and Statistics* 49 (1967): 319–331.

10. N. Fisher and J. R. Hall, "Risk and Corporate Rate of Return," *Quarterly Journal of Economics* 83 (1965): 79–92.

11. J. R. Kimberly, "Organizational Size and the Structural Perspective: A Review," *Administrative Science Quarterly* 21 (1976): 571–579.

12. F. M. Scherer, *Industrial Market Structure and Economic Performance* (Chicago: Rand McNally & Co, 1980).

13. R. M. Barefield and E. E. Comiskey, "The Accuracy of Analysts' Forecasts of Earnings per Share," *Journal of Business Research* (July 1975): 241–252.

14. Thomas E. Copeland and J. Fred Weston, *Financial Theory and Corporate Policy,* 3rd edition (Reading, Mass.: Addison-Wesley, 1992).

15. Rivera, "Prediction Performance of Earnings Forecasts: The Case of U.S. Multinationals," op. cit.

REFERENCES

Adler, M., and B. Dumas. "International Portfolio Choice and Corporation Finance: A Synthesis." *Journal of Finance* (June 1983): 925–984.

Albrecht, W. S., O. Johnson, L. L. Lookabill, and D.J.H. Watson. "A Comparison of the Accuracy of Corporate and Security Analysts' Forecasts of Earnings: A Comment." *The Accounting Review* (July 1977): 736–740.

Allen, L. ''Return and Risk in International Capital Markets.'' *Columbia Journal of World Business* (Summer 1982): 3–23.

Baginski, S. P. ''Intraindustry Information Transfers Associated with Management Forecasts of Earnings.'' *Journal of Accounting Research* (Autumn 1987): 196–216.

Baldwin, B. A. ''Segment Earnings Disclosure and the Ability of Security Analysts to Forecast Earnings Per Share.'' *The Accounting Review* (July 1984): 376–389.

Barefield, R. M., and E. E. Comiskey. ''The Accuracy of Analysts' Forecasts of Earnings per Share.'' *Journal of Business Research* (July 1975): 241–252.

Beaver, W. H., R. Clarke, and W. F. Wright. ''The Association between Unsystematic Security Returns and the Magnitude of Earnings Forecast Errors.'' *Journal of Accounting Research* 1 (1979): 316–340.

Brown, L. D., R. L. Hagerman, P. A. Griffin, and M. E. Zmijewski. ''Security Analyst Superiority Relative to Univariate Time-Series Models in Forecasting Quarterly Earnings.'' *Journal of Accounting and Economics* (January 1987): 61–87.

Brown, P., G. Foster, and E. Noreen. *Security Analysts Multi-Year Earnings Forecasts and the Capital Markets.* Studies in Accounting Research No. 21 (Sarasota Fla.: American Accounting Association, 1985).

Collins, J. Markham. ''A Market Performance Comparison of U.S. Firms Active in Domestic, Developed, and Developing Countries.'' *Journal of International Business Studies* 21 (1990): 289–300.

Copeland, Thomas E., and J. Fred Weston. *Financial Theory and Corporate Policy,* 3rd edition (Reading, Mass.: Addison-Wesley, 1992).

Elton, E. J., M. J. Gruber, and M. Gultekin. ''Expectations and Share Prices.'' *Management Science* (September 1981): 975–987.

Errunza, V. R. ''Emerging Markets: A New Opportunity for Improving Global Portfolios.'' *Financial Analysts Journal* (September–October 1983): 51–58.

Errunza, V. R. ''Gains from Portfolio Diversification in Less Developed Countries' Securities.'' *Journal of International Business Sudies* (Fall–Winter 1977): 83–99.

Errunza, V. R., and L. W. Senbet. ''The Effects of International Operations on the Market Value of the Firm: Theory and Evidence.'' *Journal of Finance* (May 1981): 401–417.

Fisher, N., and J. R. Hall. ''Risk and Corporate Rates of Return.'' *Quarterly Journal of Economics* 83 (1965): 79–92.

Fried, Dov, and Dan Givoly. ''Financial Analysts' Forecasts of Earnings: A Better Surrogate for Market Expectations.'' *Journal of Accounting and Economics* 4 (1982): 85–108.

Givoly, Dan, and Joseph Lakonishok. ''The Information Content of Financial Analysts' Forecasts of Earnings.'' *Journal of Accounting and Economics* (December 1979): 165–185.

Gonedes, N. J., N. Dopuch, and S. H. Penman. ''Disclosure Rules, Information Production, and Capital Market Equilibrium: The Case of Forecast Disclosure Rules.'' *Journal of Accounting Research* (Spring 1976): 89–137.

Hall, M., and L. Weiss. ''Firm Size and Profitability.'' *Review of Economics and Statistics* 49 (1967): 319–331.

Imhoff, E. A., Jr., and G. J. Lobo. ''Information Content of Analysts' Composite Forecast Revisions.'' *Journal of Accounting Research* (Autumn 1980): 541–554.

Imhoff, E. A., Jr., and P. V. Pare. ''Analysis and Comparison of Earnings Forecast Agents.'' *Journal of Accounting Research* (Autumn 1982): 429–439.

Kimberly, J. R. ''Organizational Size and the Structural Perspective: A Review.'' *Administrative Science Quarterly* 21 (1976): 571–579.

Levy, H., and M. Sarnat. ''International Diversification of Investment Portfolios.'' *American Economic Review* (September 1970): 668–675.

Patell, James M. ''Corporate Forecasts of Earnings per Share and Stock Price Behavior: Empirical Tests.'' *Journal of Accounting Research* (Autumn 1976): 246–276.

Penman, S. H. ''An Empirical Investigation of the Voluntary Disclosure of Corporate Earnings Forecasts.'' *Journal of Accounting Research* (Spring 1980): 132–160.

Rivera, Juan M. ''Prediction Performance of Earnings Forecasts: The Case of U.S. Multinationals.'' *Journal of International Business Studies* 22 (1991): 265–288.

Scherer, F. M. *Industrial Market Structure and Economic Performance* (Chicago: Rand McNally & Co, 1980).

Van Agtamael, A. W., and V. R. Errunza. ''Foreign Portfolio Investment in Emerging Securities Market.'' *Columbia Journal of World Business* (Summer 1982): 58–60.

Waymire, G. ''Additional Evidence on the Information Content of Management Earnings Forecasts.'' *Journal of Accounting Research* (Autumn 1984): 703–718.

APPENDIX 4.A: SAMPLE OF FIRMS

Group 1 (DO)

1. Archer-Daniel
2. Conagra
3. Emerson Elec.
4. Gannett
5. Grumman
6. Hershey
7. Int. Paper Co.
8. James River Co.
9. Kerr-McGee
10. Knight-Ridder
11. Mapco
12. Mead
13. Northrop
14. Ogden
15. PPG Ind.
16. Sherwin-Williams
17. Times Mirror
18. Union Camp
19. Westvaco
20. Whirlpool
21. Williams Co.

Group 2 (DD)

1. Air Prod. & Chem.
2. Am. Brands
3. Amoco
4. Armstrong World
5. Boeing
6. Bristol-Myers
7. Cabot
8. Compaq
9. Corning Glass
10. Ethyl
11. FMC
12. General Dynamics
13. General Motor
14. General Signals
15. H. J. Heinz Co.
16. Ingersoll-Rand
17. Johnson Controls
18. Litton Ind.
19. Lockheed
20. McDonnell Douglas
21. Minnesota Mining & Mfg.
22. Monsanto
23. Paccar
24. Phillip Morris
25. Pitney Bowes
26. Raytheon
27. Reynolds Metals
28. Rockwell Intl.
29. Rohm & Haas
30. Textron
31. Upjohn

Group 3 (DG)

1. Abbot Lab.
2. Am. Home Prod.
3. Cynamid
4. Armco
5. Avon Products
6. Borden
7. Cooper Inds.
8. CPC Intl.
9. Dow Chemical
10. Du Pont
11. Eaton
12. Exxon
13. General Electric
14. Gillette
15. Hercules
16. Honeywell
17. HP
18. Kellogg
19. Kimberly-Clark
20. Merck
21. Motorola
22. Pfizer
23. Quaker Oats
24. Schering-Plough
25. Warner-Lambert
26. Xerox

5

Multinationality, Diversification Strategy, and Ownership Structure

INTRODUCTION

A search for the variables associated with the observed differences in performance among multinational enterprises (MNE) is an important international research topic. Empirical evidence on the issue leads to results supporting the importance of a diversification strategy and internationalization for MNE performance.[1,2] The impact of ownership structure or concentration of stockholdings on this relationship has not been examined. One school of thought argues that the distribution of ownership has important implications for corporate efficiency and strategic development.[3] This chapter suggests that the economic relationships between MNE corporate performance, on one hand, and diversification strategy and internationalization, on the other hand, are best examined in the context of ownership differences between firms and develops and tests a model that describes the influence of internationalization, diversification strategy, and ownership structure on MNE corporate performance in France.

THEORETICAL FRAMEWORK

Geringer, Beamish, and daCosta[4] examined the effects of diversification strategy and internationalization on the MNE performance of the

100 largest MNEs from the United States and Europe. Diversification strategy and degree of internationalization, two fundamental elements of any MNE's strategy, involve two aspects: range and relatedness of products and relative emphasis on foreign versus domestic operations. Both diversification (measured by Rumelt's[5] classification scheme) and degree of internationalization (measured by the ratio of a company's foreign subsidiaries' sales to its total worldwide sales) were found to be significantly related to MNE 1977–1981 performance (measured by the ratio of net annual profit to sales).

Kim, Hwang, and Burges[6] examined the same relationships for sixty-two U.S. multinationals. The results were that the corporate profit performance impact of related and unrelated diversification varies, contingent on the extent of a firm's international market diversification. To measure both the product and the international market dimensions of diversification, they relied on a measure that extends the Jacquemin-Berry[7] entropy measure of diversification into the global context. Performance was measured by profit growth and stability.

This study expands on previous research along the following four lines. First, the effects of ownership structure or concentration of stockholdings are added to examine the relationship in the context of ownership differences between firms. Second, to control for country effect, the sample was limited to French MNEs. Third, dual strategy diversifiers were included in the analysis. Fourth, both direct and interaction effects of diversification structure and internationalization were examined.

The model indicates that the ownership structure, as expressed by stock concentration; diversification strategy, as expressed by both related and unrelated diversification; and internationalization influence corporate profit performance of French firms. The model assumes an interaction between diversification and internationalization.

STOCK CONCENTRATION AND PERFORMANCE

The separation of ownership and control in the large corporation causes owners' motivations to differ from those of managers. The assumption is that the shareholders, as value maximizers, view managers' responsibility to be the maximization of efficiency. Shareholders need to be able to both coordinate action and demand information that will enable them to overcome any information asymmetries and to influence management's decisions and responsibility toward value maximization and strategies that are in the best interest of stockholders. One solution for shareholders is to increase their share of stock ownership. Accordingly, higher ranges of stock ownership will be positively related to performance.

> H_1: There will be a positive relationship between performance of French MNEs and higher ranges of stock concentration.

DIVERSIFICATION AND PERFORMANCE

The strategic management literature differentiates two different types of diversification strategies: related and unrelated. Related diversifiers diversify predominantly within their industries, whereas unrelated diversifiers diversify predominantly across industries. Empirical results on the M-form hypothesis differentiated between the impact of related and unrelated diversification on performance with mixed results.[8] Lower economic returns[9,10] and lower risk[11] were found, however, to be associated more with unrelated diversification than related diversification.[12] Because of the mixed results in previous studies, both forms of diversification are expected to be significantly associated with the performance of French firms.

> H_2: There will be a positive relationship between, on one hand, performance of French MNEs and, on the other, related and unrelated diversification.

INTERNATIONALIZATION AND PERFORMANCE

Various studies support a positive relationship between the degree of internationalization and performance. Various explanations are given to include the arguments that internationalization (a) yields competitive advantages by permitting a firm to exploit the benefits of performing more activities internally; (b) enables the firm to capitalize on proprietary parent firm skills, highly developed but underutilized; (c) enables a firm to exploit interrelationships between different segments, geographical areas, or related industries; and (d) creates economies of scope, scale, and ex-

Degree of Internalization

Due to the unavailability of data, it was not possible to use the preferred ratio: foreign subsidiaries sales to total MNE sales.[16] The degree of internationalization was first measured by the ratio of a firm's international sales to total MNE sales.[17] Firms were then classified as highly internationalized if their ratio was higher than or equal to 0.44, the mode of the distribution of the ratio in the sample, or low internationalization if their ratio was lower than 0.44. The dichotomization is accomplished to treat internationalization as a class variable in the covariate analysis.

Diversification Measures

The choice of diversification measure is crucial to the empirical investigation of performance implications of corporate diversification strategy and ownership structure. Given Montgomery's results[18] on the strengths and weaknesses of the index approaches used by industrial organization researchers and the categorical approach used by strategy researchers, Palepu[19] relied successfully on the Jaquemin-Berry measure.[20] This entropy measure is used in this study.

Given a firm operating in N industry segments the entropy measure of total diversification DT is defined as follows:

$$\mathrm{DT} = \sum_{i=1}^{n} P^i \ln (1/P^i),$$

where P^i is the share of the ith segment in the total sales of the firm.

The related diversification measure DR is defined as follows:

$$\mathrm{DR}^j = \sum_{i=j}^{n} P^{ij} \ln (1/P^{ij}),$$

where P^{ij} is defined as the share of the segment i of group j in the total sales of the group.

The total related diversification measure DR is a function of DR^j. It is defined as follows:

$$DR = \sum_{j=1}^{n} DR^j P^j,$$

where P is the share of the jth group sales in the total sales of the firm.
The unrelated diversification DU is computed as follows:

$$DU = \sum_{j=1}^{n} P \ln (1/P^j).$$

Values of DR and DU are computed from data derived from the *French Company Handbook 1990.*

Covariate Variables

Two covariate variables were used to control for possible intervening effects. Assets as a measure of size were used as a covariate. Previous research has considered assets as a control measure for return on assets and variability of return on assets. The natural logarithm of 1988 assets served as a measure of size. The logarithmic transformation was used because (a) size is highly skewed and extreme values strongly affect correlations with other variables and (b) a logarithmic transformation closely approximates the normality assumption underlying the methods used in this chapter.

The age of the company was also used as a covariate. It is used to control for the potential bias toward newly diversified firms into new international market areas. Experience in international markets precedes dircct involvement in international markets, which justifies the use of the age of the company rather than the number of years in international markets. The age of the company was computed as 1988 minus the year of the founding of the company as disclosed in *French Company Handbook 1990.*

This study did not control for industry effects. The large French related and unrelated diversified firms, all highly diversified, represented thirteen major industrial sectors, so industry effects would tend to cancel out.

RESULTS

Exhibit 5.1 presents the overall results for the rate of return on assets (ROA). The results suggest that the relationships between performance

Exhibit 5.1
Results of the Analysis of Covariance for the Return on Assets

Source	DF	MS	F	P
Model	8	0.0020	3.70	0.0070*
Internationalization			2.93	0.1000***
Related Diversification			6.73	0.0166*
Unrelated Diversification			3.30	0.0828***
Stock Concentration			2.93	0.1000***
Internationalization x Related Diversification			1.79	0.1951
Internationalization x Unrelated Diversification			8.77	0.0072
Covariates				
Size (log of Assets)			3.14	0.09***
Age of the Firm			0.33	0.57
Error	22	0.00055		
Total	30			

*Significant at X = 0.00.
***Significant at X = 0.0.

and internationalization, performance and diversification strategy, and between strategy-internationalization interactions and performance are statistically congruent with past research. The type of diversification strategy, the degree of stock concentration, and the level of internationalization are systematically related to performance. An interesting result of this study is the significant interaction between unrelated diversification and internationalization. It suggests that both variables act in concert for an improvement of performance of French MNEs. The significant levels of the covariates indicate that size was an important control.

A comparison of the adjusted ROA means for high and low internationalized firms yielded a significant difference (t = 2.07387) in favor of the highly internationalized firms. ROA was 0.047 for the high group and 0.0333 for the low group.

All these results are in support of each of the three hypotheses.

DISCUSSION

The central proposition in this study is that the difference in the performance levels of French firms that employ the different strategic approaches of related and unrelated diversification is best examined in the context of differences in the ownership structure or concentration of holdings.

Hypothesis 1 was confirmed, suggesting that performance of French firms is better with higher stock concentration, which enables shareholders to align managers to the best interests of shareholders. It confirms the Berle and Means thesis[21] that the dispersion of shareholders' ownership allows managers holding little equity in the firm to forego value (wealth) maximization and use corporate assets to benefit themselves rather than the shareholders. The high stock concentration in the French case imposed the appropriate discipline on managers' behavior. Hypothesis 1 also confirms the thesis that if managers have small stockholdings, they will work toward value maximization as a result of factors including market discipline, for example, the managerial labor market, and the product market, and the market for corporate control.

Hypothesis 2 was also confirmed, suggesting that performance of French MNEs is positively related to both related and unrelated diversification. It confirms findings in other contexts and other countries about the impact of diversification strategy on the performance of MNEs.

Hypothesis 3 was also confirmed, suggesting that performance of French MNEs is positively related to the degree of internationalization. It adds to similar evidence with U.S. and/or European MNEs.

The significant interaction effect between unrelated diversification and internationalization shows that the performance gains in French MNEs arising from internationalization are best accomplished with unrelated diversification. It allows firms to exploit interrelationships between different segments in different geographical areas and unrelated industries. Internationalization increases the firm's capacity to exploit different opportunities in different markets and in different countries. This finding in the French context is very much compatible with other findings that unrelated diversification can be associated with favorable profit performance when firms are well diversified internationally.

Obviously, more research is needed to verify the results of this study in other periods and other contexts. Additional variables that may influence the relationships examined in this study need to be considered. Firms in other European markets could be included in the sample along with dummy variables to control for firm effects. A comprehensive measure of global diversification introduced in Vachani[22] also needs to be used. It was not used in this study because of the nonavailability of data. Vachani's measures are presented in Appendixes 5.A and 5.B. Finally, performance measures should include both ROA and stock value to assess the potential differential impact.

NOTES

1. J. Michael Geringer, Paul W. Beamish, and Richard daCosta, ''Diversification Strategy and Internationalization: Implications for MNE Performance,'' *Strategic Management Journal* 10 (1989): 109–119.
2. W. Chan Kim, Peter Hwang, and William Burgers, ''Global Diversification Strategy and Corporate Profit Performance,'' *Strategic Management Journal* 10 (1989): 45–57.
3. Ahmed Belkaoui and Ellen Pavlik, ''The Effects of Ownership Structure and Diversification Strategy on Performance,'' *Managerial and Decision Economics* 13 (1992): 343–352.
4. Geringer, Beamish, and daCosta, ''Diversification Strategy and Internationalization: Implications for MNE Performance,'' op. cit.
5. R. P. Rumelt, *Strategy, Structure and Economic Performance* (Cambridge, Mass.: Harvard University Press, 1974).
6. Kim, Hwang, and Burgers, ''Global Diversification Strategy and Corporate Profit Performance,'' op. cit.
7. A. P. Jacquemin and C. H. Berry, ''Entropy Measure of Diversification and Corporate Growth,'' *The Journal of Industrial Economics* (June 1979): 359–369.
8. Belkaoui and Pavlik, ''The Effects of Ownership Structure and Diversification Strategy on Performance,'' op. cit.
9. H. K. Christensen and C. A. Montgomery, ''Corporate Economic Performance: Diversification Strategy Versus Market Structure,'' *Strategic Mangement Journal* 2 (1981): 327–343.

10. R. P. Rumelt, "Diversification Strategy and Profitability," *Strategic Management Journal* 3 (1982): 359–365.

11. R. A. Bettis and V. Mahajan, "Risk/Return Performance of Diversified Firms," *Strategic Management Journal* 2 (1981): 379–393.

12. Ahmed Riahi-Belkaoui, "Diversification Strategy and Economic Performance of French Firms," *Advances in International Accounting* 5 (1992): 163–171.

13. Ibid.

14. International Business Development, *French Company Handbook 1990* (Paris: International Business Development, 1990).

15. Ibid.

16. Alan M. Rugman, "European Multinationals: An International Comparison," in M. Klaus and W. H. Staehle (Eds.), *European Approaches to International Management* (New York: Walter de Gruyter, 1986), 32–56.

17. John M. Stopford, *The World Directory of Multinational Enterprises, 1982–1983* (New York: Free Press, 1985).

18. C. Montgomery, "The Measurement of Firm Diversification: Some New Empirical Evidence," *Academy of Management Journal* 25 (1982): 299–307.

19. K. Palepu, "Diversification Strategy, Profit Performance and the Entropy Measure," *Strategic Management Journal* 6 (1985): 239–255.

20. Jacquemin and Berry, "Entropy Measure of Diversification and Corporate Growth," op. cit.

21. A. A. Berle and G. C. Means, *The Modern Corporation* (New York: Macmillan, 1932).

22. Sushil Vachani, "Distinguishing between Related and Unrelated International Geographic Diversification: A Comprehensive Measure of Global Diversification," *Journal of International Business Studies* 22, no. 2 (1991): 307–322.

REFERENCES

Amit, R., and J. Livnat. "Diversification and the Risk-Return Tradeoff." *Academy of Management Journal* 3 (1989): 154–165.

Belkaoui, Ahmed R., and Ellen Pavlik. "The Effects of Ownership Structure and Diversification Strategy on Performance." *Managerial and Decision Economics* 13 (1992): 343–352.

Bergsten, C. F., T. Horst, and T. H. Moran. *American Multinationals and American Interests* (Washington, D.C.: Brookings Institution, 1978).

Berle, A. A., and G. C. Means. *The Modern Corporation* (New York: Macmillan, 1932).

Bettis, R. A. ''Performance Differences in Related and Unrelated Diversified Firms.'' *Strategic Management Journal* 2 (1981): 379–393.

Bettis, R. A., and V. Mahajan. ''Risk/Return Performance of Diversified Firms.'' *Strategic Management Journal* 2 (1981): 379–393.

Buhner, Rolf. ''Assessing International Diversification of West German Corporations.'' *Strategic Management Journal* 8 (1987): 25–37.

Christensen, H. K., and C. A. Montgomery. ''Corporate Economic Performance: Diversification Strategy versus Market Structure.'' *Strategic Management Journal* 2 (1981): 327–343.

Dubin, M. *Foreign Acquisitions and the Spread of the Multinational Firm* (New York: Arno Press, 1980).

Fama, E. F. ''Agency Problems and the Theory of the Firm.'' *Journal of Political Economy* 88 (1980): 288–307.

Fisher, N., and J. R. Hall. ''Risk and Corporate Rate of Return.'' *Quarterly Journal of Economics* 83 (1969): 79–92.

Galbraith, J. K. *The New Industrial State* (New York: New American Library, 1974).

Geringer, J. Michael, Paul W. Beamish, and Richard C. daCosta. ''Diversification Strategy and Internationalization: Implications for MNE Performance.'' *Strategic Management Journal* 10 (1989): 109–119.

Gordon, R. A. ''Ownership and Concentration as Incentive to Corporate Executives.'' *Quarterly Journal of Economics* 54 (1940): 34–56.

Hall, M., and L. Weiss. ''Firm Size and Profitability.'' *Review of Economics and Statistics* 49 (1967): 319–331.

Hart, O. D. ''The Market Mechanism as an Incentive Scheme.'' *Bell Journal of Economics* 14 (1983): 366–382.

Hill, C. W., and S. A. Snell. ''Effects of Ownership Structure and Control on Corporate Productivity.'' *Academy of Management Journal* 32 (1989): 25–46.

Hoskisson, R. E. ''Multidivisional Structure and Performance: The Contingency of Diversification Strategy.'' *Academy of Management Journal* 30 (1987): 625–644.

International Business Development. *French Company Handbook 1990* (Paris: International Business Development, 1990).

Jacquemin, A. P., and C. H. Berry. "Entropy Measure of Diversification and Corporate Growth." *The Journal of Industrial Economics* (June 1979): 359–369.

Jensen, M., and M. Ruback. "The Market for Corporate Control: The Scientific Evidence." *Journal of Financial Economics* 11 (1983): 5–50.

Kim, W. Chan, Peter Hwang, and William P. Burgers. "Global Diversification Strategy and Corporate Profit Performance." *Strategic Management Journal* 10 (1989): 45–57.

Kimberly, J. R. "Organization Size and the Structuralist Perspective: A Review." *Administrative Science Quarterly* 21 (1976): 571–597.

Marris, R. *The Economic Theory of Managerial Capitalism* (London: Macmillan, 1964).

Mason, E. S. "The Apologetics of Managerialism." *Journal of Business* 31 (1958): 22–33.

Monsen, R. J., and A. Downs. "A Theory of Large Managerial Firms." *Journal of Political Economy* 73 (1965): 44–65.

Montgomery, C. "The Measurement of Firm Diversification: Some New Empirical Evidence." *Academy of Management Journal* 25 (1982): 299–307.

Palepu, K. "Diversification Strategy, Profit Performance and the Entropy Measure." *Strategic Management Journal* 6 (1985): 239–255.

Pfeffer, J., and G. R. Salancik. *The External Control of Organizations: A Resource Dependence Perspective* (New York: Harper and Row, 1978).

Porter, M. *Competitive Advantage: Creating and Sustaining Superior Performance* (New York: Free Press, 1985).

Riahi-Belkaoui, Ahmed R. "Diversification Strategy and Economic Performance of French Firms," *Advances in International Accounting* 5 (1992): 163–171.

Rugman, Alan M. "European Multinationals: An International Comparison." In M. Klaus and W. H. Staehle (Eds.), *European Approaches to International Management* (New York: Walter de Gruyter, 1986), 32–56.

Rugman, Alan M. *International Diversification and the Multinational Enterprise* (Lexington, Mass.: Lexington Books, 1979).

Rumelt, R. P. "Diversification Strategy and Profitability." *Strategic Management Journal* 3 (1982): 359–365.

Rumelt, R. P. *Strategy, Structure and Economic Performance* (Cambridge, Mass.: Harvard University Press, 1974).

Stopford, John M. *The World Directory of Multinational Enterprises, 1982–1983* (New York: Free Press, 1985).

Vachani, Sushil. ''Distinguishing between Related and Unrelated International Geographic Diversification: A Comprehensive Measure of Global Diversification.'' *Journal of International Business Studies* 22, no. 2 (1991): 307–322.

Williamson, O. E. *The Economics of Discretionary Behavior: Managerial Objectives in a Theory of the Firm* (Englewood Cliffs, N.J.: Prentice-Hall, 1964).

APPENDIX 5.A: DEFINITION OF TOTAL GLOBAL DIVERSIFICATION

Consider a firm that operates in:

M industries (*j*), each comprising one or more related business (product) segments (*i*), and

N country clusters (*a*), each comprising one or more similar countries (*c*).

Let P_{icaj} be the proportion of the firm's sales in the *i*th business (product) segment in the *c*th country in the *a*th region, in the *j*th industry, to the firm's total sales.*

$$P_{icaj} \geq 0 \text{ and } \sum_{j=1}^{M} \sum_{a=1}^{N} \sum_{c \in a} \sum_{i \in j} P_{icaj} = 1$$

Then the firm's total global diversification *TGD* can be defined as:

$$TGD = \sum_{j=1}^{M} \sum_{a=1}^{N} \sum_{c \in a} \sum_{i \in j} P_{icaj} \ln(1/P_{icaj})$$

Total global diversification can be split into four components:

1. Unrelated Product Diversification (*UPD*), which measures the firm's diversification across unrelated industries.

$$UPD = \sum_{j=1}^{M} P_j \ln(1/P_j)$$

   where P_j is the proportion of the firm's sales in the *j*th industry to the firm's total sales.
2. Unrelated International Geographic Diversification (*UGD*), which measures the firm's diversification across unrelated country clusters.

$$UGD = \sum_{j=1}^{M} P_j \sum_{a=1}^{N} P_{aj}^{j} \ln(1/P_{aj}^{j})$$

   where $P_{aj}^{j} = P_{aj}/P_j$ and P_{aj} is the proportion of the firm's sales in the *a*th region in the *j*th industry to the firm's total sales.
3. Related International Geographic Diversification (*RGD*), which measures diversification across similar countries within homogeneous country clusters.

$$RGD = \sum_{j=1}^{M} P_j \sum_{a=1}^{N} P^j_{aj} \sum_{c \in a} P^{aj}_{caj} \ln(1/P^{aj}_{caj}),$$

where $P^{aj}_{caj} = P_{caj}/P_{aj}$, and P_{caj} is the proportion of the firm's sales in the cth country in the ath region in the jth industry to the firm's total sales.

4. Related Product Diversification, (RPD), which measures the firm's diversification across related products

$$RPD = \sum_{j=1}^{M} P_j \sum_{a=1}^{N} P^j_{aj} \sum_{c \in a} P^{aj}_{caj} \sum_{i \in j} P^{caj}_{icaj} \ln(1/P^{caj}_{icaj}),$$

where $P^{caj}_{icaj} = P_{icaj}/P_{caj}$.

Now, $UPD + UGD + RGD + RPD$

$$= \sum_{j=1}^{M} P_j \ln(1/P_j) + \sum_{j=1}^{M} P_j \sum_{a=1}^{N} P^j_{aj} \ln(1/P^j_{aj}) + \sum_{j=1}^{M} P_j \sum_{a=1}^{N} P^j_{aj} \sum_{c \in a} P^{aj}_{caj} \ln(1/P^{aj}_{caj}) +$$

$$\sum_{j=1}^{M} P_j \sum_{a=1}^{N} P^j_{aj} \sum_{c \in a} P^{aj}_{caj} \sum_{i \in j} P^{caj}_{icaj} \ln(1/P^{caj}_{icaj})$$

$$= \sum_{j=1}^{M} P_j \ln(1/P_j) + \sum_{j=1}^{M} P_j \sum_{a=1}^{N} (P_{aj}/P_j) \ln(P_j/P_{aj}) +$$

$$\sum_{j=1}^{M} P_j \sum_{a=1}^{N} (P_{aj}/P_j) \sum_{c \in a} (P_{caj}/P_{aj}) \ln(P_{aj}/P_{caj}) +$$

$$\sum_{j=1}^{M} P_j \sum_{a=1}^{N} (P_{aj}/P_j) \sum_{c \in a} (P_{caj}/P_{aj}) \sum_{i \in j} (P_{icaj}/P_{caj}) \ln(P_{caj}/P_{icaj})$$

$$= \sum_{j=1}^{M} [P_j \ln(1/P_j) + \sum_{a=1}^{N} P_{aj} \ln P_j + \sum_{a=1}^{N} P_{aj} \ln(1/P_{aj})] +$$

$$\sum_{j=1}^{M} \sum_{a=1}^{N} \sum_{c \in a} P_{caj} \ln(P_{aj}/P_{caj}) + \sum_{j=1}^{M} \sum_{a=1}^{N} \sum_{c \in a} \sum_{i \in j} P_{icaj} \ln(P_{caj}/P_{icaj})$$

$$= \sum_{j=1}^{M} [P_j \ln(1/P_j) + P_j \ln P_j + \sum_{a=1}^{N} P_{aj} \ln(1/P_{aj})] +$$

$$\sum_{j=1}^{M} \sum_{a=1}^{N} \sum_{c \in a} P_{caj}[\ln P_{aj} + \ln(1/P_{caj})] +$$

$$\sum_{j=1}^{M} \sum_{a=1}^{N} \sum_{c \in a} \sum_{i \in j} [P_{icaj} \ln P_{caj} + P_{icaj} \ln(1/P_{icaj})]$$

$$= \sum_{j=1}^{M} \sum_{a=1}^{N} P_{aj} \ln(1/P_{aj}) +$$

$$\sum_{j=1}^{M} \sum_{a=1}^{N} \sum_{c \in a} P_{caj} \ln P_{aj} + \sum_{j=1}^{M} \sum_{a=1}^{N} \sum_{c \in a} P_{caj} \ln(1/P_{caj}) +$$

$$\sum_{j=1}^{M} \sum_{a=1}^{N} \sum_{c \in a} P_{caj} \ln P_{caj} + \sum_{j=1}^{M} \sum_{a=1}^{N} \sum_{c \in a} \sum_{i \in j} P_{icaj} \ln(1/P_{icaj})$$

$$= \sum_{j=1}^{M} \sum_{a=1}^{N} \sum_{c \in a} \sum_{i \in j} P_{icaj} \ln(1/P_{icaj})$$

$= TGD.$

*Note that instead of sales some other measure of size could be used depending on the purpose of the research. For example, if the impact of diversification on organization structure is being studied, it may be more appropriate to use number of people deployed in each business-country combination. In the past, researchers have measured international geographic diversification using sales (e.g., Rugman [1979]; Geringer et al. [1989]), number of employees (e.g., Caves, Porter, Spence and Scott [1980]; Kim et al. [1989]) and value of assets (e.g., Horst [1972]; Caves [1974]).

Source: Sushil Vachani, ''Distinguishing between Related and Unrelated International Geographic Diversification: A Comprehensive Measure of Global Diversification,'' *Journal of International Business Studies* 22, no. 2 (1991): 317–319. Reprinted with permission.

APPENDIX 5.B: BEHAVIOR OF THE TOTAL GLOBAL DIVERSIFICATION MEASURE

Given below are examples of the values the components of the Total Global Diversification measure would take for varying product and geographic configurations. The examples are for a firm based in Korea and range from a firm with fully domestic operations in one product (*TGD*=0) to one that has operations in eight product-country combinations (*TGD*=2.03). Note that the firm's domestic (Korean) operations are included in the computation in the same way as its Taiwanese operations.

The minimum possible *TGD* is zero, since ln 1 is zero; signifying no diversity in products and countries. The maximum possible *TGD* is a function of the number of product-country combinations. (Assuming three countries and three products the maximum possible *TGD*=2.19.) The higher the product-country combinations, the higher the *TGD*. This allows comparison of the relative total dispersion of the activities of different firms. Some researchers may wish to divide a firm's *TGD* by the maximum possible *TGD* to obtain a measure that falls between 0 and 1 to assess the extent to which a firm's activities are spread uniformly across products and countries.

Distribution of Sales (Percentage of Sales)										Diversification Measure				
Asia						Europe				UPD: UNRL UNRL PRD DIV	RPD: REL REL PRD DIV	UGD: UNRL INT GEO DIV	RGD: REL INT GEO DIV	TGD: TOTAL GLOBAL DIV
Korea			Taiwan			Britain								
Ind 1	Ind 2		Ind 1	Ind 2		Ind 1	Ind 2							
TV	VCR	Soap	TV	VCR	Soap	TV	VCR	Soap	Total					
100	—	—	—	—	—	—	—	—	100	0	0	0	0	0
60	40	—	—	—	—	—	—	—	100	0	0.67	0	0	0.67
50	33	17	—	—	—	—	—	—	100	0.45	0.56	0	0	1.01
40	33	17	10	—	—	—	—	—	100	0.46	0.50	0	0.30	1.26
30	33	17	10	—	—	10	—	—	100	0.46	0.44	0.30	0.29	1.49
25	25	20	10	—	—	10	—	10	100	0.61	0.35	0.48	0.27	1.71
20	20	10	10	10	10	10	—	10	100	0.61	0.42	0.48	0.52	2.03

Source: Sushil Vachani, "Distinguishing between Related and Unrelated International Geographic Diversification: A Comprehensive Measure of Global Diversification," *Journal of International Business Studies* 22, no. 2 (1991): 319–320. Reprinted with permission.

APPENDIX REFERENCES

Caves, Richard E. ''Causes of Direct Investment: Foreign Firms' Shares in Canadian and United Kingdom Manufacturing Industries.'' *Review of Economics and Statistics* (August 1974): 279–293.

Caves, Richard E., Michael E. Porter, A. Michael Spence, and John T. Scott. *Competition in the Open Economy* (Cambridge, Mass.: Harvard University Press, 1980).

Geringer, J. Michael, Paul W. Beamish, and Richard C. daCosta. ''Diversification Strategy and Internationalization: Implications for MNE Performance.'' *Strategic Management Journal* 10 (1989): 109–119.

Horst, Thomas E. ''Firm and Industry Determinants of the Decision to Invest Abroad.'' *Review of Economics and Statistics* 54 (August 1973): 258–266.

Kim, W. Chan, Peter Hwang, and William P. Burgers. ''Global Diversification, Strategy and Corporate Profit Performance.'' *Strategic Management Journal* 10 (1989): 45–57.

Rugman, Alan M. *International Diversification and the Multinational Enterprise* (Lexington, Mass.: Lexington Books, 1979).

6

Multinationality and Corporate Financing

INTRODUCTION

The observed cross-sectional difference in corporate policy decision is still an open research question needing answers. A general argument made in the field of finance is that the answer rests on the differential contracting costs.[1,2,3,4] Gaver and Gaver[5] use the contracting cost thesis to suggest an association between a firm's investment opportunity set and corporate policy choices. As stated by Smith and Watts:

> In making investment and employment decisions, however, firms invest in specialized physical and human capital. These firm-specific investments result in variation in firms' investment opportunity sets (i.e., their prospective investment opportunities and associated pay off distinctions). Corporate taxes and regulation also vary across firms. Thus, the investment opportunity set, regulation, and corporate tax provisions offer the potential to explain cross-sectional policy variations.[6]

The literature provides different measures of the investment opportunity set, which are, at best, arbitrary and ad hoc. This chapter proposes instead to measure the investment opportunity set by the degree of multinationality and determine its potential association with corporate finance polices.

THE ASSOCIATION BETWEEN MULTINATIONALITY AND CORPORATE POLICY VARIABLES

Multinationality as a Better Measure of the Investment Opportunity Set

Because the firm is a combination of assets in place and future investment options,[7] discretionary expenditures are assumed to affect only the value of the investment or growth options.[8] Examples of growth options include capacity expansion projects, new product introductions, acquisition of other firms, investment in brand name through advertising, and even maintenance and replacement of existing assets.[9] The notion of growth option is better explained as follows:

> This notion of a growth option is broader than the conception held by many academicians, who tend to envision growth opportunities solely in terms of new projects supported by extensive research and development activities, and imagine growth firms as small, struggling, start-up enterprises headed by investors—founders in white lab coats. The broader construct that we describe is perhaps better termed ''flexibility'' to avoid the more limited popular connotations of growth options. Although small, start-up firms can have abundant options to take on new projects or restructure existing assets, large, well-established firms are not barred from such opportunities. In fact, more established firms often have advantages over their smaller fees in their ability to exploit emerging opportunities.[10]

The investment opportunities differ between firms leading to cross-sectional variations in the investment opportunity set. Variables explaining the differences in the investment opportunity set include (a) the dependence of the value of investment options on the specific assets to which they are attached[11]; (b) the different firm-specific investments in physical and human capital[12]; and (c) the creation of barriers to entry through generation of economies of scale, product differentiation, brand loyalty factors,[13] or through the choice of lines of business.[14] The differences in the investment opportunity sets, added to differences in regulation and corporate financial policy with the verified propositions that growth firms have significantly lower debt-equity ratios, lower dividend yields, higher level of cash compensation to their executives, and higher incidence of stock option plans than nongrowth firms.

Testable Propositions

The diversity of the measures used is only the result of the fact that the investment opportunity set is assumed to be imperfectly observable and likely to be imperfectly measured by a single empirical proxy.

The thesis of this chapter differs from the related research by arguing that the investment opportunities are observable and best measured in terms of multinationality of a firm. Basically, the higher the level of multinationality, the greater the investment made by the firm in creating new products and potential barriers to entry. Multinationality, and its related expenditures, is one of the best examples of discretionary expenditures available to support growth options and is relevant for all industries. With respect to financing policy, firms with significant growth opportunities in terms of multinationality are expected to have higher debt-equity ratios, because equity-financing measures may be more difficult and constraining. The same growth firm may still be assumed to pursue a low-dividend payout policy given that investment and dividends are linked through the firm's cashflow identity. As generally assumed, contractual arrangements encourage firms without profitable investment opportunities to pay higher dividends rather than engage in negative net-present-value projects.

Accordingly, the testable proposition relating the corporate policy variable to multinationality as the investment opportunity set can be summarized as follows: In terms of multinationality, growth firms have higher debt-equity ratios than nongrowth firms.

MEASURING THE INVESTMENT OPPORTUNITY SET AS MULTINATIONALITY

Related Measures on the Investment Opportunity Set

To measure the investment opportunity set the following variables were used:

1. the ratio of book value of assets to total firm value,
2. the ratio of market value of equity to book value of equity,
3. the earnings-price ratio,
4. the research intensity defined by research and development expenditures/total assets or research and development/sales,
5. revenue volatility,
6. variance of the rate of return as an index of investment opportunities, and
7. the number of growth-oriented mutual funds holding the firm's shares.

All these measures are ad hoc and may not necessarily measure the investment opportunity set that is unobservable in the first place. Add to that the possible interdependence between policy decisions and investment opportunity decisions. As stated by Baker,

> In the final analysis, all of a firm's policy decisions are interdependent, and the investment opportunity set for a firm is a choice variable for the firm's management. Current actions that managements take affect the future investments that the firm can make, and are affected by the firm's leverage, dividend, and compensation policies. The board of directors, with or without external pressure, may intentionally change a firm's policy in order to induce management to adjust the investment opportunity set. Thus, there is a fundamental simultaneity in this problem that is extremely difficult to sort out.[15]

Measure of Multinationality

This chapter adopts a different strategy by looking at the investment opportunity set as the growth options existing in the multinational ventures of the firm. Hence, the investment opportunity set is best measured by the degree of multinationality.

To date, the following measures of multinationality have been proposed:

1. foreign sales/total sales,
2. research and development intensity,
3. advertising intensity,
4. export sales/total sales,
5. foreign profits/total profits,
6. foreign assets/total assets,
7. overseas subsidiaries/total subsidiaries,
8. top management's international operations, and
9. a combination of the preceding eight measures.

Because of data availability this chapter relies on the following sum measures of multinationality:

1. foreign sales/total sales,
2. foreign profits/total profits,
3. foreign assets/total assets, and
4. the sum of the preceding three measures.

THE SAMPLE

The "most international" 100 manufacturing and service firms ranked by *Forbes* from 1987 to 1992 were included as a total sample for the study.

THE DATA

The empirical analysis in the chapter concerns the association between growth in multinationality and corporate policy variables.

The financing policy variables were computed as (a) book value of debt/equity or (b) market value of debt/equity.

The definition of the financing policy variables are summarized as:

1. Book debt/equity: Total liabilities − (Total common equity + Carry value of preferred stock) and
2. Market debt/equity: Total liabilities − (Share outstanding × Share closing price + Carrying value of preferred stock).

THE RESULTS

The empirical tests consist of regressing each of the policy variable on a dummy variable representing growth opportunities (GROW) in the multinational areas and two controls of variables, namely, the logarithm of assets and return in market value (ROM) measured as operating income divided by market value. The variable GROW takes the value of 1 if the firm is in the growth sample and 0 otherwise. The growth (nongrowth) sample consists of firms whose level of multinationality is in the top (bottom) 25 percent of the distribution where the level of multinationality is measured by one of the following four measures: (a) foreign revenues/total revenues, (b) foreign profits/total profits, (c) foreign assets/total assets, and (d) the sum of the last three measures.

Exhibit 6.1 presents the results. The policy variable is in column 1. Next to the policy variable, the letters a, b, c, and d refer to the measure of multinationality used: a, for foreign revenues/total revenues; b, for foreign profits/total profits; c, for foreign assets/total assets; and d, for the sum of the last three measures.

As predicted, the results indicate a positive relationship between debt financing and the growth factor of multinationality, both when the debt-equity ratio is measured by the book value and by the market value. Both firm size and return on market value are significant controlling variables. Overall, the results provide evidence that after controlling for firm size and performance, growth firms in terms of multinationality have higher debt-equity ratios than nongrowth firms.

CONCLUSIONS

The chapter provides evidence on the cross-sectional structure of basic financing policy choices. It shows that growth firms in terms of multinationality have significantly higher debt-equity ratios than nongrowth firms, after controlling for firm size and firm performance. It adds to the

Exhibit 6.1
Coefficients for Firm Policy Variables

Variables	N(1)	intercept	Grow(2)	ROMV(3)	LAssets	R2	F
Debt/Equity (book) a.	355	-27.92 (-9.23)	1.45 (1.92)*	-2.81 (-1.2)*	3.37 (11.35)*	26.97	43.33*
Debt/Equity (book) b.	394	-30.42 (-10.76)	2.96 (3.97)*	-8.46 (-4.1)*	3.69 (12.84)*	34.57	68.85*
Debt/Equity	344	-29.72	1.44	-1.90	3.59	31.34	51.87*
Debt/Equity (book) d.	354	-31.52 (-10.71)	3.24 (4.14)*	-7.72 (-2.9)*	3.78 (12.9)*	34.77	62.3*
Debt/Equity (market) a.	356	-31.81 (-10.38)	1.16 (1.71)*	-5.39 (-2.4)*	3.68 (12.21)*	30.40	51.38*
Debt/Equity (market) b.	395	-36.77 (-10.38)	2.21 (2.37)*	-18.62 (-5.4)*	4.35 (12.06)*	34.62	70.72*
Debt/Equity (market) c.	345	-29.67 (-9.03)	0.05 (0.08)*	-18.62 (-5.4)*	3.66 (11.39)*	32.35	54.51*
Debt/Equity (market) d.	355	-35 (-1.03)	9.27 (2.58)*	-30.6 (-10)*	4.21 (12.57)*	43.94	91.98*

(1) Number of observations.

(2) Grow = growth dummy variable taking the value of 1 if the firm is in the growth sample and 0 otherwise. The growth (nongrowth) sample consists of firms whose level of multinationality is in the top (bottom) 25 percent of the distribution, where level of multinationality is measured by (a) foreign revenues/total revenues, (b) foreign profits/total profits, (c) foreign assets/total assets, and (d) the sum of the last three measures.

(3) ROMV = return in market value as operating income/market value of the firm.

(4) LAssets = log of total assets.

evidence showing systematic relations between the firm's investment opportunity set and other corporate policy decisions. However, whereas previous studies showed a negative relationship between financing policy and the investment opportunity set, this chapter shows that the relationship is instead positive if multinationality is used to measure the growth options implied by the investment opportunity set.

NOTES

1. M. C. Jensen and W. H. Meckling, "Theory of the Firm: Management Behavior, Agency Costs and Ownership Structure," *Journal of Financial Economics* 3 (1976): 305–306.
2. S. Myers, "Determinants of Corporate Borrowing," *Journal of Financial Economics* 5 (1977): 147–175.
3. F. Easterbrook, "Two Agency Cost Explanations of Dividends," *American Economic Review* 24 (1984): 650–659.
4. M. S. Rozeff, "Growth, Beta and Agency Costs as Determinants of Divided Payout Ratios," *Journal of Financial Research* 5 (1982): 249–259.
5. J. J. Gaver and K. M. Gaver, "Additional Evidence on the Association between the Investment Opportunity Set and Corporate Financing, Dividends and Compensation Policies," *Journal of Accounting and Economics* 16 (1993): 125–160.
6. C. W. Smith and R. L. Watts, "The Investment Opportunity Set and Corporate Financing, Dividend and Compensation Policies," *Journal of Financial Economics* 32 (1992): 142.
7. Myers, "Determinants of Corporate Borrowing," op. cit.
8. S. Kole, "An Investigation of the Bundling of Compensation Plans," Working Paper, University of Rochester, 1994.
9. S. P. Myers and R. C. Merton, "The Role of Contigent Claims Analysis in Corporate Finance," in E. Heliman (ed.), *Recent Advances in Corporate Finance* (Homewood, Ill.: Iiri, 1985), 7–54.
10. Gaver and Gaver, "Additional Evidence on the Association between the Investment and Corporate Financing, Dividends and Compensation Policies," op. cit.
11. W. C. Kester, "An Options Approach to Corporate Finance," Chapter 9, in E. I. Altman (ed.), *Handbook of Corporate Finance* (New York: Wiley, 1986), 3–35.

12. Smith and Watts, ''The Investment Opportunity Set and Corporate Financing, Dividend and Compensation Policies,'' op. cit.

13. K. Chung and C. Charaenwong, ''Investment Options, Assets in Place, and the Risk of Stocks,'' *Financial Management* 20 (1991): 21–33.

14. A. Christie, M. Joye, and R. Watts, ''Organization of the Firm: Theory and Evidence,'' Working Paper, University of Rochester, 1989.

15. G. P. Baker, ''Growth, Corporate Policies, and the Investment Opportunity Set,'' *Journal of Accounting and Economics* 16 (1993): 164.

REFERENCES

Gaver, J. J., and K. M. Gaver. ''Additional Evidence on the Association between the Investment Set and Corporate Financing, Dividends and Compensation Policies.'' *Journal of Accounting and Economics* 16 (1993): 125–160.

Myers, S. ''Determinants of Corporate Borrowing.'' *Journal of Financial Economics* 5 (1977): 147–175.

Smith, C. W., and R. L. Watts, ''The Investment Opportunity Set and Corporate Financing, Dividend and Compensation Policies.'' *Journal of Financial Economics* 32 (1992): 122–142.

Index

About the Author

AHMED RIAHI-BELKAOUI is Professor of Accounting at the University of Illinois at Chicago. He is the author of many Quorum titles, including his most recent *Accounting, A Multiparadigmatic Science* (1996).

ISBN 1-56720-077-X
90000>
EAN
9 781567 200775
HARDCOVER BAR CODE